Trains in Transition

IN THE GREAT TRADITION

Classic and immaculate, and in dramatic fulfillment of the most spectacular heritage of American railroading, a tandem of the Pennsylvania Railroad's K 4s Pacific locomotives surges over the mainline west with seventeen cars of the Spirit of St. Louis, crack de luxe flyer on the New York–St. Louis run. The K 4s Pacific type engine is the standard motive-power over most of the Pennsylvania's steam-operated divisions and both a road engine and helper are required to maintain the Spirit's speedy schedule, as shown here near Vandalia, Illinois.

LUCIUS BEEBE

TRAINS IN TRANSITION

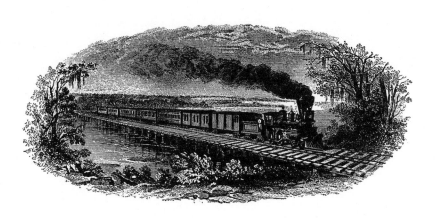

BONANZA BOOKS • NEW YORK

This edition is published by Bonanza Books,
a division of Crown Publishers, Inc.
by arrangement with the original publishers,
D. Appleton-Century Company, Inc.
(E)

To the little railroads of the land which maintain as valiantly as Class 1 carriers the tradition and legend of the high iron, this book is inscribed

Lucius Beebe photograph

Contents

INTRODUCTION 1

1 HOTSHOT 11

2 THE DIESEL DREAM 81

3 VARNISH VIGNETTES 143

4 SUPER DE LUXE 165

Railroad Photographs

Illustrations

The Spirit of St. Louis . . . . *frontispiece*
Pontchartrain . . . . *title-page*
Milk for Manhattan . . . . *page* v
Texas Pacific Blueblood vii
With Booster Working ix
The Pause That Refreshes 1
Gulf, Mobile Action 4
Rolling into Altoona 7
Merchandise South 9
Nickel Plate Redball 11
Class S 2 on the Milwaukee 19
Wabash Superpower 20
On the Advertised 21
Santa Fe Type, Burlington Owned 22
He's Got Green Ahead 23
High Cars, West 23
Tandem on the Colorado Hills 24

PAGE

Frisco Hotshot, Carrying Green 25
Narrow-gage Archetype 26
Streamlined Freight Power 26
Into the Sunset 27
Southland Superpower 28
White Flag for Loveland 28
Mikado Tandem 29
Light Monon Haul 30
Carrying Green, Kaysee Bound 31
Rock Island Roundhouse Pride 32
Fast Burlington Merchandise 32
C. & E. I. Freight Power 33
Prototypal 2-10-2 34
First Section, B. & O. 35
The Railroad Redivivus 36
Working Steam out of Madison 37
Steel and Iron Camel 38
The Mopac Pulls Its Freight 39
Triple Shotted for the Grade 40
Drag on the Northern Pacific 41
Double Header in a Hurry 41
Almost to Timberline 51
Peddling His High Cars 52
In Tennessee Pass 53
Wintertime Pastoral 53
More Than a Mile of Train 54
At the End of the Run 55
"Noble and Nude and Antique" 56
Mike on the Inland 56
Memorial to an Empire Builder 57
Titan of the U. P. Trail 58
The Newsboy on Its Rounds 59
The Cotton Belt's No. 19 60
B. & O. Behemoth 60
St. Johnsbury and Lake Champlain 61
Mike on the C. & E. I. 62
Miniature Hotshot 63
High Cars East 63
Reading Superpower 64
Ready for Orders 65
Canadian Pastoral 66
"A Mallet and a Million" 67
One-spot in Action 68
Rolling the Empties 68
Mighty Power on the Espee 69
Rare in Eastern Railroading 70

PAGE

Big Power on the Big Four 71
Alton and Southern in Action 72
Ozark Dawn 73
Alton Auxiliary Tank 79
Rolling out of Denver 81
This Train Sold the Bill of Goods 87
Transition on the Q 88
Companion to the Dixieland 89
The Bluebonnet 90
Vintage Sprinter 90
Versatile and Sightly 91
"Divides the Desert and the Sown" 92
"Made Up of Wheels, the New Mechanic Birth" 93
A Century of the Pony Express 93
The Merchant's Limited 94
Along the Lehigh Valley 95
Vanishing Race 96
Steam, Streamlining and Seacoast 97
"His Heart a Spinning Coil, His Juices Burning Oil—" 98
Wonder and Glory of the Mopac 99
Thunder on the Hudson 100
Sleek and Silver Trimmed 101
Diesel on the Alton 102
Seaboard at Sunset 103
Era's End 104
An Era Ends and Begins Here 113
The 400 in Transition 114, 115
Veteran of the Diesel Generation 116
Study in Streamlining 117
Old Timer on the C. & E. I. 118
The Santa Fe in Colorado 119
Eastbound from St. Louis 119
A Veteran of the Iron 120
Reeling Off the Colorado Miles 121
Leaving Denver Behind 121
A Silver Greyhound Steps Out 122
Orange, Silver, Purple and Gold Trim 123
Graveyard Run 124
Rocky Mountain Blueblood 125
On the Commuting Run 125
No Pantograph Rises Here 126
Far Cry from Link and Pin 127
No Transcendent Beauty 128
High in the Raton 128
"Fleeter of Foot than the Fleet-foot Kid" 129
In Deepest Essex County 130

                                                                    PAGE
Cinderella of the Rails 131
The Prospector 141
Narrow Gage at Santa Fe 143
Collector's Item 147
Old Timer of the Rails 148
Veteran High Stepper 149
Ancient of Railroading Days 149
In a Class by Itself 150
Over the Top of the World 151
B. & M. Western Division 152
Right Out of Yesterday 152
Illinois Central's Crack Varnish 153
The Whistler of the Boxcars 154
Before the Streamliners Came 155
Illinois Pastoral 156
Santa Fe Smoke 157
Never Again to Georgetown 158
Crack Cotton Belt Varnish 159
99-I, Classic Pennsy Electric Power 160
Blue Bird in Flight 161
Camelback Fireboy 163
R. F. & P. Varnish North 165
Up from the Ozarks 169
These Made Railroad History 170, 171
Doll House Train 172
The Super Chief 173
The Panama Limited 174
Speed for the Bankers and Brokers 175
In the Vale of Bethel 175
On the Banks of the Ohio 176
The Central's Southwestern 177
In the Legendary Sierras 178
Covers the Old Wild West 179
Rio Grande Local 180
The Robert E. Lee 181
Crack Texan Flyer 181
The Golden State Limited 182
Carrying White on the M. & St. L. 183
"She Was Working Steam with Her Brake Shoes Slack" 184
How Times Do Change! 185
Monster of the Coal Pits 185
Modification on the Union Pacific 186
"In That New World Which Is the Old, And O'er the Hills and Far Away!" 191
Belle of the South 192
In the Modern Manner 193
Headed for Far Horizons 194

PAGE

The Broadway Comes Home 195
Drifting into Palm Springs 196
Racing for Chicago 197
Mopac Superpower 197
Full of Years and Honors 198
Along the Alton 199
K4s in Modern Dress 200
Among the Latter-Day Saints 201
Main Line West 201
Service for the Chief 202
Big Power for the Big Four 203
The Vanishing Ten-Wheeler 204
Nearing Its Terminal 205
Louisville and Nashville Mike 205
Typical of Canadian Railroading 206
Headed South Rapidly 207
Ninety an Hour on the Milwaukee 210

Introduction

TO THE gratification of the precise minded and to amateurs of the symmetrical period, the history of American railroading has arranged itself almost exactly in cycles of a century. Whatever point of departure one may select for the chronicle of rail transport: the inaugural run of the Best Friend of Charleston, the construction of the Baltimore and Ohio's locomotive Atlantic or the adoption of the longitudinal boiler in the design of the engine York in 1837, automotive railroad operation through the agency of the steam expansion engine had its origins in the early years of the fourth decade of last century and the cycle of steam lasted almost precisely one hundred years without essential modification or the evolution of any important competitive type of motive power. For ten decades and without challenge or questioning railroad history, practice and progress were postulated on the inescapable and demonstrated circumstance that water transformed into steam occupies sixteen hundred times its original space.

Whether this scientific axiom was illustrated in the Camden and Amboy's John Bull, in the graceful Taunton-built eight wheelers of the sixties and seventies or in the Atchison, Topeka and Santa Fe's Northern type locomotives that to-day power its varnish hauls from La Junta to Los Angeles, a distance of 1235 miles, without change, the coefficient of the expansion of steam was the Mosaic law upon which was built in its entirety the legend of overland steam and steel in America.

The conquest of the American continent has been, in essence, a triumph of steam railroading, sharing its bay wreaths only with such allied agencies as the magnetic telegraph, the Sharp's rifle, the Mississippi River packet and Colt's Frontier Model Peacemaker revolver. The bravura interludes of a national epic, the scaling of the High Sierras by virtue of the mortmain of Theodore Judah, the forensic and Albert

3

Lucius Beebe photograph

watch chain glories of Promontory, the first Atchison and Topeka cattle hauls powered over the Raton and Glorieta by almost as many wood burning eight wheelers as there were high cars in a given train, the coda to all anabases against the hills played in terms of empires and millions by David Moffatt, were all of them orchestrated to the gleaming passage of crossheads in their immutable guides and a thousand main rods slamming down in their augment on the bonded iron which reached from sea to sea.

The emergence upon the transportation scene of an entirely new type of motive power was not quite unheralded. There was, for example, the development of power lines maintaining a feed of energy into electrically propelled locomotives of proven economy and practicability. Two circumstances militated against any widespread adoption of electric railroading, however: it is economically practicable only where there is such density of traffic as is characteristic of very few divisions of only a handful of carriers, and its installation—mile for mile—is almost precisely as costly as the construction of an entire new railroad.

But, foreshadowed or not, the appearance in 1934 of Diesel-electric locomotives designed as a serious consideration for long distance passenger hauls was managed by its instigators with a maximum of dramatic overtones, and its impact, together with that of its allied catchword, "streamlining," upon the public consciousness was immediate and considerable. Unquestionably "streamlining" was a second shot in the arm of the railroad industry along with air conditioning which saved passenger travel from almost complete obliteration at the hands of rival agencies. One was practical and the other tickled the general fancy.

"Streamlining" has by no means been adapted only to trains motivated by Diesel-electric power, but, generally speaking, lightweight equipment, airflow design and Diesel-electric locomotives have become closely associated in the public mind and the association has been adroitly furthered by a number of interested parties. This circumstance, more than the conviction that universal change in styles of motive power is in immediate prospect, has occasioned the title of this book.

The bid, through the multiple new attractions of passenger service: luxury extra-fare transcontinental varnish trains, de luxe coach flyers, accelerated schedules and attractive tariffs, for a return of public trust and esteem by the railroads has only been the window dressing for the real revolution that has characterized the last transportation decade. Vast gains in operating efficiency, improved methods of signaling and despatching, the construction of long haul locomotives and the necessary adjustments in fuel facilities, and enormously heavier rails, have brought all classifications of freight service to a condition which was regarded as the ultimate perfection in passenger service in the middle twenties.

To-day fast blocks of Florida fruit and vegetables reach New York for third morning markets; export livestock is handled over 800 miles within the 36-hour limit ordained by law; the produce of California rolls over the High Sierras and the wastelands of Nevada and Utah on guaranteed schedules for delivery in Chicago and the east; coal is now a high speed commodity, and overnight deliveries in the Middle West have been so stepped up with hotshot merchandise trains thundering across the midnight countryside that waybills must be telegraphed ahead.

The drama of modern railroading is being written by such passenger-speed redballs as the New Haven's Speed Witch, the Central's Merchandiser, the Santa Fe's No. 39 on the Chicago-Kansas City run, the Southern Pacific's Overnight, powered between Los Angeles and San Francisco by the proudly varnished, streamlined passenger locomotives of the Daylight class, the M.K.T.'s Katy Packer, the Frisco's Fleet of Flashes and the more than half a hundred overnight flagships of the Burlington, Rio Grande, Erie, Illinois Central, Missouri Pacific, Pennsylvania, Seaboard, Southern, Texas and Pacific, Pere Marquette and Union Pacific.

It is the object of this book to chronicle some of the aspects of this transition. Believing that the camera is probably here to stay, it has been the intention of the author, both in this and its two companion volumes, to record the saga of American railroading as much as possible through the agency of speed or action photographs. He has always had the heart-warming coöperation of other historians and enthusiasts of the railroad legend; often he has had the coöperation of railroad executives. It is sometimes difficult for men charged with the responsibilities of railroads to understand that the public might be interested in the technique and the more dramatic aspects of their calling. The author has experienced particular hospitality at the hands of the officers of the Atchison, Topeka and Santa Fe and the Terminal Railroad Association of St. Louis. He has inevitably been extended head-end courtesy by the first and is authorized to operate the motive power (within certain restrictions) of the other, of both of which he is inordinately proud.

There are railroads, however, whose officers are not so much pleased as they are outraged that "outsiders" should be fascinated by their art and mystery and who attempt to preserve the details of valve motion, automatic signaling and train despatching in a manner positively Druidical. Photographs showing smoke exhaust have been known to produce symptoms bordering on those of epilepsy. A menace to the safety of state and nation has been seen by many a special officer in a camera pointed at a peddler freight setting out cars of company coal on lonely sidings in Nebraska and Oklahoma, and it is a satisfaction to the author that several of his own shots in this book were made in defiance of such preposterous Dogberrys.

There are, to aficionados of railroading, trains and roads which exercise upon the imagination a fascination to the exclusion, often enough, of more important documentary material and this is true of the author as of anyone else. He is, for example, particularly fetched by the Chicago and Eastern Illinois' motive-power, much of it so ancient as to border on the obsolete, but invariably kept as spick and span as any other road might keep its most celebrated streamliner. The St. Louis Zipper, a valiant little streak of varnish on the Chicago run, might, to the non-infatuate, be quite without charm, yet the very names of the towns through which it passes have a flavor all their own: Momence, Sollitt, Watseka, Goodwine, Hustle, Westervelt, and Dollville.

There is (or was,) Train No. 1—it had no more distinguished billing than that—of the Fort Worth and Denver City which clattered overnight from the Rockies to the wealthy reaches of East Texas. It was possessed of a wonderful wooden dining car whose continual creaking and complaining constituted a sort of terrifying leitmotif to the theme of rattling plates in its kitchen. Its superstructure swayed so on curves that diners wouldn't have been in the least astonished had the roof and side

Railroad Photographs

walls finally flown completely away leaving them seated at table and consuming cutlets on the deck of a carpeted flat car.

There is the Burlington's Denver Zephyr, one of the most beautiful as well as earliest of streamliners where the author encountered a dining car steward who had once been in service as butler in his family. There was the standard weight Chief a few years ago on which he once travelled to the Coast with an English actor on his first trip to America who was sure the train would be ditched and pillaged by hostile redskins and who slept with a Webley Service revolver under his pillow against this morbid contingency. Trains have as much variety of character and association for voyagers as have ships and infinitely more, of course, than motor cars or flying machines.

By happy circumstance the age of steam railroading has lasted well into the era of still, and later, speed photography and the record is relatively complete from the time of Colonel Charles R. Savage and his wet plate chronicle of Promontory down to the present moment. It is only unfortunate that as much cannot be said for those other picturesque phases of the saga of American transportation, the clipper ships and the overland stages.

It is not beyond the reach of imagination that competition and the mutations of time will make the bravest chapters in the legend of railroading those chapters which have already been written or which are even now blending into a heroic coda. It will be the author's reward if this book and the two companion volumes which have gone before it may serve to reflect for readers past or future any of the splendors of the high iron and the men who dominated it, sometimes dangerously, always and inescapably with a panache of romance.

For their good offices in assisting the author to collect material both editorial and photographic he is indebted to a number of agencies and individuals. To Mr. Volney Fowler of the Electro-Motive Corporation and General Motors he is deeply obligated for the technical material in the chapter on Diesel-electric motive-power. To Officer William Barham of the St. Louis Police Department and his partner, Ivan Oaks, U.S.A., he owes his best thanks for some of the most dramatic railroad photographs ever taken. He has made frequent photographic safari in Illinois and Missouri with Robert A. Willier of the Wabash, who is almost as train-smitten as himself. Mr. H. W. Pontin of Railroad Photographs has been most generous in his contributions, as have been many individual photographers whose work has been credited to them, it is hoped correctly, in every instance where it has been used.

It is hoped that this book may bring some pleasure and satisfaction not alone to railroad historians and lovers, but to all who cherish the American legend in its manifold individual aspects.

L. B.

Lucius Beebe photograph

1
Hotshot

FOR MORE than ten decades they rolled the high cars behind steam power. As early as the middle thirties of the nineteenth century the seniority of passenger hauls over freight was established in operating schedules of several railroads. A full century of various practices in the handling of merchandise followed, progressing in speed and efficiency as power improved, suffering setbacks during the years of the War Between the States, undergoing a tremendous acceleration in carding and increase in train tonnage during the twenties and thirties of the present century and culminating in the passenger-schedule overnights, the hotshot fruit blocks from California and Florida, and the other speed merchandise hauls of the present moment. In the current forties coal drags a mile and a quarter long are handled with almost the urgency of the strawberry specials of twenty years ago.

And all of it was powered with steam.

To-day only one freight train in a thousand, from the world's fastest long-distance redball—the Illinois Central's famed MS-1—to the Southern Pacific's Overnights between San Francisco and Los Angeles which are powered by the road's sleekest and swiftest passenger locomotives, is other than steam powered, but there is a "clamor and rumor of things to be" in the existence of Diesel-electric super-power which will not be stilled.

Ever since the Electro-Motive Corporation, a subsidiary of General Motors, in 1933 furnished motive-power for the first Diesel-electric passenger train, its designers, engineers and research men have had in mind the development of a locomotive of the same type which would adapt its operating economies, its more or less continuous availability and its abatement of roadbed strain to the business of mainline freight hauls. In 1939 the first of Electro-Motive's 5400-horsepower freight units started service up and down the continent in demonstration runs, and two years later the Atchison, Topeka and Santa Fe put into regular freight service on one of the road's western runs an improved version of this monster of the high iron, and by the end of 1941 five such engines, each capable of powering an average 5000-ton, 100-car train for a distance of 500 miles without a fuel stop were on the Santa Fe's power roster.

While it is obvious from these small beginnings that the inaugural of what is potentially an age of Diesel is at hand, equally obviously it puts no period to the age of steam, since, even if no single order for a steam freight locomotive should ever again be placed by any railroad (and scores of such orders are being placed annually) the available supply of steam motive-power would still be serviceable for several decades. There are engines thirty and forty years old in service on a sound economic basis on many American railroads, and the longevity of locomotives has increased incalculably since the turn of the century.

Diesel-electric may be on its way in but steam is very far from being on the way out.

Even a modern railroad man cannot read the future. But the recent and immediate past—what a progressive development they presage! Not only weight and power and speed are developing apace. Not only do the freights carry their golden shipments at breath-taking speed on cross-continental journeys, but they are doing it in fancy dress. You only have to read their own advertisements—not ads to the public, but trade journal ads to shippers and railroad men—to see what side the rail-roaders are putting on nowadays. It started with the passenger trains.

With the coming of the so-called streamliners there was also notable a widespread reversion to an older tradition of American railroading, a revival of the use of color in the motive-power and equipment of crack passenger trains. The silver sheen of the Burlington Zephyrs and the yellow and brown of the Union Pacific "city" series found themselves closely followed by the blue and silver of the Century, the orange, red, and black of the Espee's celebrated Daylight, and the flaming green and yellow of the Northwestern's 400. The locomotives of the Boston and Maine started bearing names again instead of numbers, and steam power on the Wabash, Frisco and Lackawanna started to emulate the prover-bial rainbow.

To-day there is under way, as may be remarked by humble commuters as well as transcontinental voyagers, a movement to spruce up even the once drab and shabby freight equipment of the land. No freight haul yet rivals, to our knowledge, the gaudy consist of some of the crack strings of varnish, but the lines are going in for illustrating their high cars with maps, mottoes and fancier-than-usual heralds, and there is no telling where the end may be. Union Pacific box-cars announce that they belong to the road of the streamliners; Sante Fe says "Sante Fe All the Way," and prints a ten-foot square map to prove it; the Milwaukee blazons its reefers and automobile cars with the slogan, "The Route of the Hiawathas," and the Burlington is content to assert it serves "Everywhere West." The day may yet come when rolling stock in green and lavender, topaz and cerise will be commonplace.

There used to be in every railroader's lexicon the names "drag freight" and "peddler freight." There is not much need of either any more, because both are on the way out. In fact, they practically have disappeared. Speedy long-distance movement has finished off the former; coördination of fast freight with highway trucks has painlessly accounted for the latter.

Time brings great changes, the philosopher said; and he might have added, in all truth, especially to the railroads. Freight-train speed jumped from a 11.5 m.p.h. average speed in 1921 to 16.7 m.p.h. two decades later. All other averages spelling progress also expanded. Number of freight cars per train went up from 37.4 to 49.7. Net tons per train increased from 651 to 849. Gross ton-miles per freight-train hour doubled—from 15,555 to 33,808. Net ton-miles, likewise, from 7560 to 14,027. And so on. In every statistical classification, the record has been one of tremendous progress.

In the period cited, the average active freight car moved up to twelve more miles a day. The average active freight locomotive traveled twenty miles more per day. Freight-train speed increased 45.2 per cent. The average load per car for all commodities carried in carload lots on Class I railroads grew to 37.7 tons. Those are revealing figures. They indicate that more than the freight itself is in movement. They also prove that the railroads are going places.

And going fast! The improved equipment in modern, efficient rolling stock in itself is an eye-opener. For comparison's sake, look back a moment to 1932 and 1933 when purchases of new freight cars amounted to 2469 and 1761 cars, respectively. Compare them with 165,703 purchased in the first sixteen months of the fourth decade of this century. Purchase commitments mean that 1941 will account for 100,000 new freight cars; 1942, 120,000, and 1943, another 150,000. Nobody need worry that the railroads will lack carrying capacity.

Locomotive figures tell the same story. In 1932, twelve were ordered. Yes, just twelve. In the early part of this decade, the railroads are buying locomotives at the rate of 1250 annually.

Not only numbers, but degree standards are playing a part in the improvement of the railroad freight situation. Equipment is being renewed at an astonishing rate, but an entirely new standard of efficiency is being set. On some railroads, the number of miles operated between shoppings of both cars and locomotives have been so lengthened that the increase reaches to 350 per cent. The result to shippers' convenience is easily realized: fewer delays because of engine failure, less need for use of rip tracks in terminals for repairs under load, less likelihood of transfer of the lading!

To an old railroad man—the fellow who now sits on his front porch, enjoying his pension and watching the trains go by—what has happened between world wars, so to say, presents a picture which makes him wonder if he is dreaming or awake. It just does not seem real. One can imagine him mouthing the phrase, "Hotshot coal and ore."

"It don't make sense," he readily could say. But it is fact. Miracle fact, maybe, but true as rain. Nowadays they take coal overnight from mine to tidewater. It was no wishful thinking on the part of mine owner or city merchant that brought this about. On the contrary, it was the leading coal- and ore-handling roads, with a vision of service to be rendered, who spent millions in improving their roadway, their rolling stock, and their coal- and ore-handing facilities. The vision they saw and the courage they had in laying on the line the money needed to operate their vision, made it possible to take coal and ore out of the drag class of traffic and put it in the hotshot class.

And even the ex-railroader ought to be the last to say it can't be done. Because the railroads never have admitted that anything they could visualize was impossible to carry out. When coal and ore and lumber move more rapidly than many redball commodities of a generation ago, it is obvious that a revolution has occurred in freight transportation.

The increased tempo has taken a lot of planning and tens of millions of dollars. Better rolling stock is only one factor. Others are increased attention to track and structure maintenance, reduction of curvature, modern facilities for coaling and watering in shorter time, modern signaling, improved train despatching methods—these and a host of others.

The list would not be complete without a special emphasis on electrification, such as, for instance, the extension of electrification by the Pennsylvania, to include the freight as well as the passenger lines between New York and Harrisburg, and Philadelphia and Washington.

There is a story about how a certain overnight freight got its name which is indicative of the new attitude of the industry toward freight movement. It's about a Grand Trunk Western making the run from Chicago to Detroit, called the "Cuckoo Train."

"Why do they call it that?" a G.T. executive was asked.

"Because," was the answer, "if we're delayed only a few minutes in getting started, the boss goes cuckoo."

That attitude is the prevailing one to-day. Express freights get absolutely affectionate attention from railway operating officers and the higher-ups: the same painstaking supervision that the heavily advertised passenger flyers get. No longer may a yardmaster or any local dignitary hold a train until tonnage, power, and what-have-you suit his convenience. They leave according to scheduled time-tables, and what's more, they arrive when due. On time and right!

Engine runs up to a thousand miles are commonplace to-day. Fast merchandise trains in this day and age operate from the freight house at the initial terminal to the freight house at the final terminal without yarding en route. Coördinating with subsidiary trucking systems has been a fruitful means of eliminating stops. Fast freights are stopped only at zoning points, and from there deliveries are made via truck to adjacent territory.

Railroad chiefs get a great deal of quiet satisfaction out of what their speed achievements have been able to do for the food industry. All sections of trade benefit from time saved in shipping America's products and produce, but it needs no great stretch of imagination to realize how growers of perishables especially benefit. And, of course, the people who ultimately purchase them!

The transportation map of the country has undergone a considerable shrinkage. Reductions of twenty-four to forty-eight hours in delivery time have become almost commonplace. That is why the eastern seaboard enjoys California and Florida edibles all winter long. The railroads have contributed to this social betterment a good deal more than speed of delivery. They have developed equipment that is equivalent in service and usage and advantage to the refrigerator in a private home.

Beyond that, the steady application by the railroads of all that technology has developed has made it possible to eliminate many of the delays that used to be thought an inevitable accompaniment of freight haulage. Modern freight transportation demands that cars must be kept moving, and every factor contributing to delay has been under continuous study. Better-built equipment, better pre-inspection, better facilities along route for emergency repairs, better automatic block facilities—all preventives against delay and all aids to speed get the green light from the treasurer.

Every modern device for time saving contributes to freight speed accomplishments. Newly developed equipment shortens time for coaling locomotives and allows water to be taken simultaneously. The Sante Fe has reduced by 10½ minutes the time spent at every water stop between Chicago and Los Angeles, totaling approximately five hours.

So, too, with qualifying hard waters. Twenty years ago the Illinois Central had an engine failure (meaning one to three hours' delay) for every five thousand locomotive miles. To-day, by reason of water treatment, this has been reduced to one such engine failure every ten million locomotive miles. Elimination of stops by improved equipment and overall traffic coördination, shorter stops when made, greater improved speed (70 miles per hour over long distances)—these are the basic factors that have metamorphosed the railway freight situation. No one believes that present speeds are set. They will go higher. Perhaps a glimpse into the future will be afforded by a brief look backward.

CLASS S 2 ON THE MILWAUKEE

This handsomely proportioned 4-8-4 wheeling southward through Lake Forest, Illinois, at the head end of 110 high cars is designated in the power roster of the Chicago, Milwaukee, St. Paul and Pacific as Class S 2 to be assigned to either freight or passenger service as the occasion may demand. Capable of handling eighteen standard-weight Pullmans on the road's crack Olympian at top speeds between Minneapolis and Harlowtown, Minnesota, the forty locomotives of this design represent the best in modern dual service power to be built by Baldwin. They incorporate Boxpok cast steel driving wheels, Walschaerts valve motion with a valve travel of 7½ inches, Timken roller bearings on drive wheels and front trucks, solid steel plate pilot. Type B du Pont Simplex stokers, 74-inch drivers, 285 pounds boiler-pressure, and a tractive force of 70,800 pounds. Shown flying white flags and clipping off forty-five miles an hour, No. 216 of this series is passing through the woodlands of the celebrated Armour estate at Lake Forest.

WABASH REDBALL

There are ninety-one cars of hotshot merchandise rolling behind these two Wabash locomotives through Mitchell, Illinois, at a mile a minute. The helper engine, No. 2822, is a 4-8-2, while the road engine, No. 2910, is a 4-8-4. The train is No. 96 and the high cars are rocking as they eat up the midwestern miles.

Truman Pouncey photograph

ON THE ADVERTISED

The hogger of this Texas and Pacific 4-10-2 passenger locomotive verifies his carding on his Hamilton as he rolls twelve cars of coaches and Pullmans over the high iron between Marshall and Dallas at seventy just at dusk. Visible in this suggestive speed shot by Truman Pouncey are train speed indicator, controls for engine air and train line air, sander, throttle, and Johnson bar fixed on its quadrant at the "company notch," or position suitable for the most efficient and economical expenditure of steam power. Railroad watches are customarily twenty-one jewel movements with dials numbered in bold Arabic numerals for easy visibility and a locked position ratchet so that the hands cannot inadvertently become ungeared from the movement and cannot be set without unscrewing the dial and releasing a lever in the edge of the watchcase itself. Regulations regarding railroad watches vary with different roads. On the New York Central, for example, they must be open-faced with a minimum of nineteen jewels, adjusted to five positions and temperature variations. The maker's name must be engraved on the timepiece and a tolerance of thirty seconds a week is allowed, although few modern railroad watches vary more than five or ten seconds in that period. Inspection is required monthly. Checking on trainmen's timepieces is accomplished by a card issued by the watch inspector and carried by the trainman, who never adjusts his own watch. Heavy gold Albert watchchains are still a hallmark of the railroad profession.

Lucius Beebe photograph

SANTA FE TYPE, BURLINGTON OWNED

A 2-10-2 Burlington freight hog plods toward Denver over the northbound iron shared by the Colorado and Southern, Santa Fe, and Rio Grande. Behind the locomotive's auxiliary tank-car is a mixed consist of company coal, chemicals, and high cars of miscellaneous merchandise.

HE'S GOT GREEN AHEAD

*Upper right:
Paul H. Stringham
photograph*

It is apparent that the signals in the next block are green for this Toledo, Peoria and Western, the Effner Redball, as it approaches Eureka, Illinois, behind No. 80, a Class H-10 Northern type with the simplified lines characteristic of the road's more modern power. The photographer, Paul Stringham, is a Rock Island employee and makes a specialty of action shots of his company's equipment.

REDBALL WEST

*Lower right:
Lucius Beebe
photograph*

Through the farmlands of southern Illinois, near Highland, the Pennsylvania's daily scheduled hotshot CC 1 slams toward St. Louis with 110 carloads of mixed merchandise under a July sun. At the smoky end is one of the Pennsy's powerful Class M-1a Mountain type engines whose 250 pounds of boiler pressure and eight 72-inch drivers give it a tractive force of 64,550 pounds. On a slight downgrade, as shown in the picture, the engineer isn't working steam, but he was rolling at a good forty miles an hour when the photographer's Graflex caught him leaning from the cab window.

J. W. Maxwell photograph

TANDEM ON THE COLORADO HILLS

These two articulated giants of the Denver and Rio Grande Western—note the arrangement of the high and low pressure cylinders on the helper—are battling the grade at Lincoln Hills, Colorado, with forty-eight cars of merchandise behind them. Their twin exhausts against the mountain background of rocks and spruce make a dramatic study in western railroading.

William Barham–Ivan Oaks photograph

FRISCO HOTSHOT, CARRYING GREEN

Because of the mortality rate of dust jackets the remarkably dramatic action shot appearing on the wrapper of this volume is reproduced here where handling and the mutations of time are less likely to result in its destruction. The train is the St. Louis–San Francisco Railroad's No. 38, first section, with sixty-five cars of California perishables fighting the two per cent grade of Valley Park Hill, Missouri. Two giant 4-8-2's built in the Frisco's own shops, the helper, an oil burner, No. 4401, the road engine a coal burner, No. 4310, are rolling the consist at a mile a minute as recorded by the camera of William Barham, a traffic officer on the St. Louis police force. Few railroad photographers have as dramatically captured the romance of speed and action on the high iron.

NARROW-GAGE ARCHETYPE

Flying white flags to designate it as an extra, although there may have been no other train over the tracks for several days, this Colorado and Southern narrow-gage 2-8-0, No. 65, is running ahead of five cars of freight and a crummy in Clear Creek Canyon near Floyd Hill, Colorado.

STREAMLINED FREIGHT POWER

On the Overnights, its pioneer, dusk-to-dawn freight flyers operating on passenger schedules between San Francisco and Los Angeles, the Southern Pacific regularly assigns locomotives of the Golden State type such as also power their crack varnish runs, the Daylights and Larks. It possesses an impressive fleet of these extraordinarily handsome engines characterized by a silver, orange, and black color scheme and "skyline casing," an extension across the top of the boiler lagging of the Espee's own smoke deflector. This is the southbound Overnight running into Glendale, California, behind 4-8-4 No. 4411.

INTO THE SUNSET

Gone forever are the golden days of the narrow-gage railroad in America and the little roads are, most of them, in their last twilight. In the past few years some sixteen hundred miles of narrow-gage rails have been torn up and only about fourteen hundred remain of all the prosperous smaller-than-standard roads which came into being and flourished so bravely in the latter half of last century. Of these, 750 miles are operated by the Denver and Rio Grande Western, whose No. 454, a miniature Mike, is climbing against the setting sun at Cerro Summit, west of Cimarron, Colorado. The Grande is jointly owned by the Western Pacific and the Missouri Pacific and its hundred-ton Mikados hauling mixed consists through the Colorado Rockies, where no standard-gage road could survive economically, still show a profit.

MIKADO TANDEM

The Toledo, Peoria and Western's Nos. 42 and 43 are hotfooting it across the
Illinois countryside near Mapleton with a string of mixed cars.

SOUTHLAND SUPERPOWER

The first Mallet in America was built in 1903 for the Baltimore and Ohio with a
wheel arrangement of 2-6-6-2. To-day the Virginian operates monsters designed
with twenty drive wheels, and many other roads use them where enormous tractive effort is required rather than high speed, although the Union Pacific uses
Mallets for a variety of purposes including power for their Challengers and other
heavy passenger trains in the San Bernardino Mountains of California. This
Norfolk and Western 2-6-6-4, No. 1202 was snapped by Mr. Prince with a mile
of coal cars behind at a crossover near South Norfolk, Virginia.

WHITE FLAGS FOR LOVELAND

Loveland, Colorado, is on the Colorado and Southern between Boulder and Fort
Collins, but the Great Western Sugar Company also wanted an outlet to the
Union Pacific mainline. It therefore maintains the Great Western Railroad, whose
2-8-0, No. 60, is shown here trailing a car of coal on its branch from Eaton to
fire the refinery furnaces.

LIGHT MONON HAUL

The Chicago, Indianapolis and Louisville Railway's two main lines run between Chicago and Indianapolis and Michigan City and Louisville, crossing each other at Monon, Indiana, whence derives its popular name, the Monon Route. A brief monograph might well be written about the incorporated names of railroads in the United States, many of which are so long as to be impractical for ordinary business or conversational purposes. There is the Cleveland, Cincinnati, Chicago and St. Louis Railway, the Big Four Route of the New York Central System; there is the Atchison, Topeka and Santa Fe, known to travelers as the Santa Fe and to banking circles as the Atchison; there is the Chicago, Burlington and Quincy Railroad Company which is the Burlington to the public and the "Q" to railroad men. There was a period of railroad financing in the nineteenth century when no rail stock was considered respectable unless it contained the word "Pacific" even if its charter never provided for it to cross the Mississippi. To-day there are forty railroads with the name Chicago incorporated in their titles. As mouth-filling as any are the Cincinnati, New Orleans and Texas Pacific Railway, the Georgia Ashburn, Sylvester and Camilla Railway Company, the Murfreesboro–Nashville Southwestern Railway Company, the Spokane, Coeur d'Alene and Palouse. Shown above is a Monon Consolidation (2-8-0) veteran jogging through Englewood, Illinois, with a crummy in tow.

CARRYING GREEN, KAYSEE BOUND

The first section of the Atchison, Topeka and Santa Fe's widely advertised No. 39 is pulling slowly out of the Corwith Yards, Chicago, at six o'clock of a wintry afternoon. The power is a Mike with a maximum rating of 1600 tons and will handle the section as far as Shopton, Iowa, where another engine of the same class will take over and roll them into Kansas City at 7:30 the next morning. The on-time performance of this train with a usual consist of fifty-odd cars has been better than 97 per cent over a period of several years.

R. H. Kennedy, Jr., photograph

C. & E. I. FREIGHT POWER

More than many of the great trunk lines, the smaller roads of the Middle West have always exercised a fascination upon the author. Here, northbound out of Terre Haute, Indiana, is a Chicago and Eastern Illinois Mikado, rolling over the flat Indiana countryside with eighty cars of mixed consist.

ROCK ISLAND ROUNDHOUSE PRIDE

Upper left: Paul H. Stringham photograph

Any superintendent of motive-power would be proud of this handsome Rock Island 4-8-4, No. 5051, Class R-67b, as it breasts the grade at Sheffield Hill, near Tiskilwa, Illinois, at the head end of No. 91, the California Gold Ball.

FAST BURLINGTON MERCHANDISE

Lower left: Lucius Beebe photograph

The Chicago, Burlington and Quincy's No. 61 gets its highball out of Chicago yards at ten o'clock at night. At one the next afternoon the engineman gives it a service application of air to slow for the switches and crossovers of East St. Louis. Here No. 61 is clattering across the Illinois meadows behind Mikado No. 5312 with a modest but still respectable pay load of about thirty cars.

PROTOTYPAL 2-10-2

The Santa Fe type locomotive with its 2-10-2 wheel arrangement was so named because it was first introduced as a class of freight engine by the Atchison, Topeka and Santa Fe Railroad. Here, near Victorville in the Cajon Pass of the San Bernardino Mountains in California on the Santa Fe's mainline, the low, powerful drive wheels of No. 1691, carrying white and with safety valve popping, is heading east with a long string of mixed merchandise. A helper engine is cut in in the middle of the train and a pusher is bringing up between the way car and the last freight car.

FIRST SECTION, B. & O.

Flying green and racing for the East St. Louis yards at what would have been considered passenger-train speed a decade ago, the first section of the Baltimore and Ohio's No. 96 rolls toward the Alton and Southern crossover a few miles east of the Mississippi on the run from Cincinnati. The power is a conventional B. & O. 2-8-2, No. 4546.

Paul H. Stringham photograph

THE RAILROAD REDIVIVUS

The Minneapolis and St. Louis is one railroad that came back from the dead to confound the experts who said it could never be made a going concern again. The M. & St. L. main line extends 485 miles between Minneapolis and Peoria. A secondary main line extends 223 miles from Minneapolis to Watertown, South Dakota, with additional South Dakota mileage of 217 miles. The total mileage including branches is approximately 1500. In 1934 railroad and financial experts said the road would have to be partitioned off among the solvent lines covering adjacent territory. Six years later, under the administration of the road's president and receiver, L. C. Sprague, there were three quarters of a million dollars cash on hand, more than $13,000,000 had been expended on improvements out of earnings, 85 locomotives, 3100 freight cars and 48 passenger coaches had been scrapped and the money accruing reinvested in modern equipment and roadbed. All this during hard times. The M. & St. L. is to-day regarded as a classic example of railroad rehabilitation through modern approach to problems of operation and maintenance. Shown in the photograph is Mikado No. 609 westbound with a local freight near Peoria, Illinois.

William Barham–Ivan Oaks photograph

WORKING STEAM OUT OF MADISON

The Litchfield and Madison Railway Company operates out of St. Louis, connecting forty miles to the north at Benld, Illinois, with the Chicago and North Western and at Litchfield with the Wabash. Save for a handful of mixed runs, it is entirely a freight railway and the picture shows Redball No. 119 snaking out of Madison on the northbound run behind Mikado No. 158 with forty cars.

STEEL AND IRON CAMEL

Largest users of auxiliary water cars attached to locomotive tenders are the Texas and Pacific, Southern Pacific, Frisco, and Missouri Pacific railroads. The practice was actually inaugurated in the spacious days of the construction of the Central and Union Pacific roads, and the Jupiter arrived from California with Leland Stanford's train for the famed celebration at Promontory in May, 1869, with a tank-car, but pioneers in recent times have been the operations technicians of the Missouri Pacific. The auxiliary tank saves time and fuel in substantial quantities, eliminates water stops and does away with the elimination of chemical content in water formerly stored in certain localities in the west. Ten or fifteen thousand gallons is the usual load, and in many cases they double an engine's capacity for carrying fuel water. This huge Texas and Pacific Texas type (2-10-4) drifting into the yards at Texarkana with more than a mile of southbound freight is equipped with a tank which is visible behind its tender.

William Barham–Ivan Oaks photograph

THE MOPAC PULLS ITS FREIGHT

Most familiar to railroad photograph collectors is the Missouri Pacific's giant tribe of Mountain locomotives, largely employed in passenger service. Here is a Mopac 2-8-2, running with sixty cars as Extra 1488, northbound at a mile a minute at Dupo, Illinois.

Paul H. Stringham photograph

TRIPLE SHOTTED FOR THE GRADE

An unusual and spectacular action shot shows three Chicago and North Western heavy-duty hogs, Nos. 2803, 2514, and 2802, a Northern, Mountain, and Northern respectively, coming up out of the Illinois River Valley northwest of Peoria with 110 cars of mixed consist. Only rarely does a photographer get an action picture of three such powerful locomotives working together at the headend. On most mountain divisions the custom is to cut the power into the middle of the consist or use the helpers at the rear of the train. Note the left-hand operation characteristic of the North Western.

DRAG ON THE NORTHERN PACIFIC

A Northern Pacific Mike with a liberal portion of its guts hung ahead of its smokebox rattles ahead of eighty-four cars of mixed consist into Thompson Falls, Montana, at thirty miles an hour.

*Upper right:
J. W. Maxwell
photograph*

DOUBLE HEADER IN A HURRY

The Peoria and Eastern's No. 21 and 37, both Mikados, are rocking the high cars behind them on an Indianapolis-bound redball freight, crossing a timber trestle at a flat sixty just east of Tremont, Illinois. The Peoria and Eastern is a subsidiary of the Big Four and the legend "New York Central System" is discernible on the tenders of its engines.

*Lower right:
Paul H. Stringha
photograph*

Freight-carrying used to be dominated by thinking which evolved from James J. Hill's evaluation of factors in the service. To wit: Freight-train operating expenses vary with train-miles, so that the fewer train-miles made and the more ton-miles sold, the better the financial result. Thus there predominated slow-moving freight trains loaded to the tractive capacity of the locomotives over the ruling grades. The typical locomotive was a 2-8-2 or Mikado type. Along came the 2-8-4 type locomotive, marking the beginning of the use of higher boiler pressures. With speed constantly being accelerated, locomotive research and improvement were constant, and the Northern 4-8-4 locomotive type came into existence. Thus was met the need called for by the demand for merchandise freight trains to operate for long distances at 40 to 45 mile-an-hour schedules, requiring sustained road speeds up to 70 miles an hour.

Gradually but certainly, a change in concept was ruling freight operation. Train loading was being determined primarily by demands of the service rather than by basic requirements of economical operation.

This did not mean that the old James J. Hill formula was upset. Train-miles still cost money, and ton-miles produce it. But as speed has increased, tonnage has mounted. When the average freight speed was 10.3 miles per hour, the average gross train load was 1443 tons. With the speed going up to an average 16.7, the tonnage average has gone up to over 1900 tons.

The steam freight locomotive being built to-day may be standard for a long time to come, or it may be improved to provide still more speed. It has what not so long ago it was determined the locomotive of the future must have—boiler capacity necessary to develop high horsepower outputs at relatively high speeds with the tractive capacity necessary to move car-limit trains over ruling grades.

A railroad man or a mere railroad enthusiast could take the grandest possible busman's holiday by merely thumbing through the trade journals. What a story they tell! What enthusiasm they reveal, as the words of the advertising copy-writers chronicle the great freight moving accomplishments of the present day!

"Your freight twenty-four hours faster to California," Sante Fe shouts in print. And goes on to tell that "from Chicago, St. Louis and points west thereof, to and including our Missouri River cities, we offer twenty-four hours earlier delivery to all points in the San Francisco Bay territory, the Los Angeles metropolitan area, and San Diego." They're specific. Freight originating in the Chicago Switching District will be delivered at these California destinations, they tell you, at 7:00 A.M., sixth morning. From St. Louis, Kansas City, St. Joseph, Atchison, and Leavenworth Switching Districts, same time, fifth morning.

The Burlington cries its wares under a screaming banner headline, "Shrinking the Map of the West." They diagram it, as the historians do when they compare travel time nowadays with the eighteen days it took George Washington to go from Boston to Savannah. "In fifteen short years," says the Burlington advertisement, "freight schedules have been shortened as much as 60 per cent—and the battle against time still continues."

The Cotton Belt uses the imagery of radio broadcasting to get across the idea of speed. The flash of the transmitter pictorially links its shipping points on both sides of the Mississippi south from St. Louis, and then went to the Pacific Coast. Figuratively, you see it racing—the Blue Streak Fast Freight.

The Southern Railway lists the time schedules of its fastest freights under the simple headlined statement: "Southern's Faster Scheduled Freights Bring Northern Markets Two Days Nearer the South." No passenger traffic promotion man ever thought up nobler slogans. Here are the six the Southern advertises: Eastern Rocket, the Clipper, Southern Flash, Cottoncade, Spinning Wheel, Fabricade. The time schedule for the Southern Flash indicates the meticulous attention to schedule which to-day is typical of freight transportation. Here it is:

Lv. Potomac Yard	2.00 A	Mon.
Ar. Atlanta	11.59 P	Mon.
Ar. Birmingham	7.00 A	Tues.
Ar. New Orleans	11.05 P	Tues.

The Tuscan red banner of the Pennsylvania blazes forth in its advertising with the message that "WHEELS Are Rolling Faster." And the insertion goes on to tell you that freight flows smoother and swifter. Time in transit has been cut in half, the reader learns. Fifth and sixth morning delivery has become third morning delivery. Overnight deliveries have become standard between points four hundred miles and more apart.

The Pennsylvania tells you how it came about. "It didn't just happen." It stems from $600,000,000 spent over a decade in improvements; including electrification of the East, speeding up freight movement over the entire system; enlargement and rearrangement of many important yards; installation of heavier rail; use of new type equipment; improvements in design and power of locomotives. The ad copy makes a lot of the coördination of rail and truck transportation from which has evolved the Zone Station system of local freight service. It puts, it says, the customer in the small community on a par with the fellow in the metropolis. By it, the highway truck has replaced the old time peddler freight with a result that service is faster, more regular and less costly, and includes delivery to the consignee's door.

The New York Central's advertisements are conservative in tone, compared to some of its western colleagues, but they pack a factual punch. "175 Fast Freights Every Day," they proclaim. "Many of these freights maintain dependable top speed of seventy miles an hour by using locomotives and wheel trucks of passenger equipment type."

The nearest the New York Central lets itself come to the florid is when it mentions a few of its favorites by name. "Crack flyers," it says, "like The Merchandiser whisk your less-carload shipments between New York and Buffalo in the record time of 10 hours and 50 minutes. Nationally known swift freights like NY-8 wheel two and a half million pounds of fresh and perishable foods from Chicago to New York for third morning delivery as does SLD-6 between St. Louis and New York. Freights like BA-6 provide second morning delivery between Buffalo and Boston."

Freight time schedules printed in its advertising take in all the important shipping points of the East and Middle West. The shipper learns at a glance what he wants to know. Overnight, second morning, three days: it tells the quick story of fast time.

The Frisco Lines go in heavily for alliteration. F F F stands for Frisco Fast Freight. Featured is the Frisco Fleet of Flashes, to give, as the advertisement proclaims, "3-Way Super-Service" in the Frisco belt. The Oklahoma Flash is heralded as the fastest overnight merchandise service—St. Louis to Tulsa and Oklahoma City—via the shortest line. . . . Speed and satisfaction—Kansas City to Tulsa and Oklahoma City. The Texas Flash is announced as fast and dependable: out of St. Louis and Kansas City to-night—second morning delivery at Dallas and Fort Worth. The Dixie Flash is proclaimed the only overnight freight service from Memphis to Birmingham with direct connections to The Carolinas, Georgia, Florida, and Alabama. Frisco's newest fast freight—the Creole Flash—coördinates with Southern's Clipper and Rocket from Kansas City and St. Louis to and from New Orleans.

The time-table tells its own story:

SOUTHBOUND: (CREOLE FLASH-CLIPPER)

Lv. St. Louis	Frisco Lines	7.30 pm Mon.
Kansas City		9.30 am Mon.
Springfield		6.00 pm Mon.
Wichita		9.00 pm Sun.
Oklahoma City		9.15 pm Sun.
Tulsa		8.00 am Mon.
Ft. Smith		7.30 pm Sun.
Joplin		10.00 am Mon.
Memphis		8.20 am Tue.
Ar. Boligee		6.00 pm Tue.
Lv. Boligee	Southern Ry.	7.00 pm Tue.
Ar. New Orleans		6.45 am Wed.

Could a shipper who lived his life in the drag freight age read that and not wonder what has come over the world he knew?

It must be contagious, this form of advertising. The freight agents have got to be so modern, they jazz the spelling like folks in show business. As for instance, the "Time-Saver Service" advertising the Fast Katy Freights! There are three of them, described like this: "The Katy

Komets—a fleet of the fastest freight trains ever operated over Katy lines . . . 22½ hours from St. Louis to Fort Worth . . . second morning delivery at Houston and San Antonio on merchandise, livestock, and packing-house products . . . overnight service in both directions between Galveston, Houston, Austin and San Antonio." Then there is The Katy Packer, northbound, with its consist of livestock, packing-house products, fresh fruits and vegetables. . . . Provides Texas shippers with exceedingly fast service to Kansas City and St. Louis markets . . . with close connections for eastern and northern points. . . . Fort Worth to Kansas City in 18½ hours . . . and to St. Louis in 25¾ hours. In the third group: The Katy Klipper, the Rocket, the Bullet. "Hours slashed from schedules," says the ad, "mean more efficient service by the Katy which serves the Southwest." Like the New York Central, the Katy puts a load of emphasis on what it calls its Train-Truck Co-Ordinated Service.

The Union Pacific ads are big and commanding, but withal modest. They stress the job and the facts. One complete label, "Challenger Merchandise Service," covers everything, among which one finds "next morning delivery at points within 500 miles from jobbing centers."

The U.P.'s up-to-the-minute service is typified by a fleet of fast overnight trains equipped with specially designed merchandise cars serving the entire system. Typical runs are from Portland to Boise, 491 miles, and Salt Lake City to Las Vegas, Nevada, 450 miles—overnight.

The stretch and reach and power which fast freight effects on the American scene is to be visualized in this sober summary of Union Pacific advertising. "This . . . service," it says, "assures shippers of fast, dependable, on-time deliveries by a reliable organization which assumes complete responsibility for package merchandise, large or small, between shipper's platform and customer's door.

"Whether it's lumber or plywood from the Pacific Northwest, fruit or vegetables from the Yakima and Walla Walla valleys, oranges and grapes from California, Union Pacific high-speed transcontinental freight service assures dependable on-time deliveries. . . . Perishables travel in clean, carefully refrigerated cars, while daily authentic tracer and diversion service affords immediate diversion to other markets."

Back East, the New Haven features its Famous Four, leaders of its

Great Fleet of Freight Trains. Like all the fast freights, the cognomens make one think of almost unimaginable speed. The New Haven leads off with its Speed Witch, serving the region between Boston, southern New England, New York, and as far south as Baltimore: early morning deliveries in all instances. Next in line is the Round Up, literally labeled to indicate its later closing hour in Boston, Providence, and New York, and the assurance of early next morning deliveries. Then comes the Cannon Ball, geared for extra speed and smooth handling, because its merchandise is largely perishable. It delivers to the New York terminals and piers for transshipment south and west. And then comes the Maine Bullet, serving all New England to New York and its piers. The New Haven, too, stresses the coördination made possible by its own subsidiary motor-truck fleet, putting its service at the doors of all New England. The services of the New Haven's once celebrated fish train nightly between Boston and Manhattan have been taken over by other regularly carded freights. Its dripping high cars being switched in the middle of Atlantic Avenue at the pleasantly odorous pier heads of the waterfront were once as familiar a feature of Boston life as Parker's Hotel or the incredibly aged trainshed of the North Station.

There is a certain feeling of nostalgia produced by big, double-paged, colorful advertisements sponsored by the Rio Grande. Their theme is of progress since the gold rush days of the seventies, from the time of the narrow-gage baby road to its modern system of to-day. It is worth quoting.

"Step by step the Rio Grande and the heart of the vast Inter-mountain West have progressed together.... The six-mile Moffat Tunnel cuts through the Colorado Rockies almost a mile below the summit of James Peak. The Dotsero Cut-off reduced the rail distance from Denver to Salt Lake City via Rio Grande by 175 miles—placing the Denver Gateway to Omaha and Chicago on an even footing with the Pueblo gateway to Kansas City and St. Louis.... Less spectacular but fully as important have been the realignment of roadbed, new ballast, new ties, new rails and fastenings, new and improved signaling equipment.

"Designed especially for mountainous territory, the massive 4-6-6-4 and 4-8-4 types of Rio Grande locomotives are actually more flexible than smaller units. Their speed and tractive power roll the merchandise hotshots across Colorado and Utah."

No natural barrier has kept the railroads from adding ever more speed to the carriers of freight as the twentieth century moves along in its fifth decade. That note of advancement is sounded in a ringing advertisement by the Chesapeake and Ohio. "Progress with the will to serve is what counts in railroad transportation," is the way recent C. & O. progress is introduced. Thousands of all-steel box-cars, hundreds of all-steel caboose and flat cars, Mallet locomotives—all purchased in a single year,...new equipment in the last decade representing purchase value running into millions of dollars. The program of progress speaks of additional tracks, scales, automatic signals, cranes, new warehouses, new passing sidings, additional company telephone circuits, new turntables, increased station and yard facilities, equipping thousands of freight cars with modern air brakes, laying 33,000 tons of new 131-pound rail, and a record of 99 per cent of all equipment in good working order. "That," the road explains, "is what C. & O. means by progress—an assurance of readiness to meet current needs as well as shippers' expanding requirements."

The Chicago Outer Belt Line advertises "Around Chicago, not through it." Every twenty minutes a freight train is despatched. Motive-power in abundance . . . that's how, its advertising tells you.

To close this review of achievement let us look at the Southern Pacific. They gear their message to national defense. "Every time a railroad car or locomotive is built or track improved, America's capacity for National Defense is increased." In eighteen months, more than $43,000,000 has gone into new equipment. Forty giant Articulated Consolidation locomotives (wheel arrangement 4-8-8-2) are in for a cost of $8,500,000. These serve both passenger and heavy-duty, high-speed freight use. They bring the S.P. number of these unique cab-in-front engines up to the impressive total of 203. The same advertisement also lists thirty new streamlined Golden State type locomotives—the engines that pull the famous Daylights and the overnight freight between San Francisco and Los Angeles: $5,500,000 worth!

"From Portland, Oregon to New Orleans in Louisiana; from San

Francisco to Ogden, 70,000 Southern Pacific men and women are working night and day to speed the movement of goods for National Defense;
to see that vital materials are delivered when and where they are wanted.
Lumber from the Northwest to build Army camps, copper from Arizona,
sulphur from Texas and Louisiana, iron ore from Utah ... heavy, carload trains roaring over mountains and across deserts, helping to make
America strong. . . . Merchandise trains, too. Thirty-six Southern Pacific
overnights link principal centers in the West and South. Moving on passenger-train schedules, they carry machines and parts for National
Defense. These overnights are coördinated with 6578 miles of track lines,
serving thousands of communities."

Thus the record runs. To the old time boomer, or home guard either,
for the matter of that, who risked life in side door cabooses and with
link and pin, who was innocent of the benefits of hog law, and who
worked trains with a maximum of thirty cars and had to cut his trains
on the ruling grades at that, the notion of naming a freight train and
running on passenger carding would have been little more than an opium
dream, as unsubstantial in potential reality as the Happy Valley Railroad of high iron mythology.

Railroads have been spending at the rate of a half-billion dollars per
year since the twentieth century moved into its fifth decade, and that
sum is exclusive of expenditures for cars and locomotives. It is mainly for
enlarging and improving the basic plant. And why have they done it?
The answer may be given in a single word. Speed. To chop hours and
even days from freight schedules.

The improvement has been country wide. No section has a monopoly
on fast freight service.

Let us look in some detail into the record of acceleration. Start by
looking south. The Southern's Cottoncade has cut twenty-four hours
from Greenville, South Carolina to Pinners Point, Virginia. Likewise with
the Fabricade from the textile mill territory in the Carolinas to New
York. With the Frisco, a similar time-saving is made between St. Louis–
Kansas City to New Orleans. Ditto for the Clipper between Cincinnati
and New Orleans.

The high-speed winter-run perishable train via the Florida East Coast gives third morning delivery in New York on traffic from main line points as far south as Fort Pierce, Florida. The Seaboard operates numerous overnights between terminals three hundred miles and more from many busy southern terminals. It has speeded up the delivery of Georgia's peaches to New York so that they arrive at 11 P.M. the first day after loading instead of the second morning. The Atlanta, Birmingham and Coast has made a distinct contribution to the fast perishable schedules between Florida and the north. The same story may be told of the Central of Georgia.

On the Atlantic Coast Line, Trains 208 and 207 have been speeded up between Augusta, Georgia, and Richmond to an overall speed of 34 m.p.h. for the 465-mile run. Fast overnight services from Atlanta to South Carolina points and from Richmond to North and South Carolina points have averaged from forty to sixty cars each.

First morning deliveries are being made by the Louisville and Nashville for distances up to four hundred miles, and second morning deliveries for distances up to a thousand miles. Trains 71 and 79 leaving St. Louis and Cincinnati respectively at the close of the day's business arrive at Nashville, three hundred miles, at 6 A.M. There they are consolidated and give first afternoon delivery, five hundred miles distant, at Birmingham; and second morning delivery at Mobile, Pensacola, New Orleans, nine hundred miles.

The Gulf, Mobile and Ohio, since the consolidation of the G. M. & N. with the M. & O., has revised its schedules for improved service to shippers.

Now take a look at the transcontinental service, modern, improved style. The Canadian Pacific has reduced by a full day the schedule between Calgary and Winnipeg. The Northern Pacific, with connections, has cut a day between Chicago and the Pacific Coast. The Union Pacific has participated in the twenty-four-hour-earlier delivery at all Pacific and north Pacific Coast points. Its numerous overnights operate over distances up to 491 miles. Its livestock run, Denver to Chicago, 1034 miles, is negotiated in thirty-four and a half hours. On the Southern Pacific, the schedule from Chicago to the Pacific Coast has been cut to the sixth morning; from St. Louis to the fifth morning. Its freight overnights have

ALMOST TO TIMBERLINE

In the High Sierras above Truckee and a few miles west of the California-Nevada border, the Southern Pacific's Sunday local No. 295 on the Reno-Frisco run is briefly posed against a skyline of mountain bleakness and desolation. Starting at Sparks, Nevada, two miles east of Reno, the local is powered by one of the Espee's famed cab-first mallets as it works westward over the Donner Pass and around Cape Horn until it heads down the long winding miles of the old Central Pacific's route to Sacramento and, finally, Oakland. The cab-foremost, articulated locomotives were evolved by the Southern Pacific as motive-power for this particular run to obviate the smoke menace to head-end crews in the tunnels and snowsheds of the run and to give the engineer a clear view on the sharp curves of mountain divisions. In this action shot the fireman is shown looking back to estimate his fire from the oil smoke exhaust behind him.

Lucius Beebe photograph

PEDDLING HIS HIGH CARS

Throughout the middle and southwest, where terrains are generally level and ruling grades negligible, the Mikado is the favored locomotive type for freight hauls of moderate tonnage. Where mile-long hotshots on speed schedules are carded, such giant power as the Frisco's Mountain types and the Texas and Pacific's 2-10-4s are favored. Here is a veteran Burlington Mikado ahead of a peddler freight whose consist of a dozen high cars and tanks is rattling down the speedway a few miles north of Granite City, Illinois.

IN TENNESSEE PASS

Readers of that admirable periodical, *Trains,* have seen this striking action shot of Denver and Rio Grande Western freight power high in the winter hills of Colorado near Mitchell in the Sawatch Mountains. Engine 3602 is a Class L-131, 2-8-8-2 articulated and, with a similar helper at the rear, can move a 48-car train up a 3 per cent grade at 15 miles an hour. Their combined tractive force is close to 264,000 pounds. Mr. Kindig has secured here one of the most dramatic of all photographs of mountain railroading.

Upper right: R. H. Kindig photograph

WINTERTIME PASTORAL

Second No. 7, the Frisco's Bluebonnet, with an overflow of holiday mail from the first section raises the finely powdered snow southbound at Valley Park Hill, Missouri. The engine is a standard design Frisco 4-8-2, hustling to keep on schedule a few miles behind the first section.

Lower right: William Barham —Ivan Oaks photograph

MORE THAN A MILE OF TRAIN

Stretching out into the distance with approximately 125 feet of slack between engine drawbar and caboose (slack averages approximately one foot per freight car) in this train are 125 cars of mixed consist clattering down the Pennsylvania's mainline at Princeton Junction, New Jersey, at thirty miles an hour. The two electric locomotives serving as road engine and helper are both Class P-5a with a 4-6-4 wheel arrangement, one streamlined with a steeple type cab, and the other an older model with box type cab. P-5a is standard electric power on the Pennsylvania, designed for use either in freight or passenger service and in single or multiple units depending upon the requirements of the individual assignment. It is a single phase locomotive, weighing approximately 195 tons and generating a continuous horsepower of 3750.

William Barham–Ivan Oaks photograph

AT THE END OF THE RUN

The St. Louis–San Francisco's fast overnight freight No. 832, the Memphis Flash, crosses the Mermac River near Ten Brook, Missouri. This overnight redball between Memphis and St. Louis is powered by a sleek 2-8-2, No. 4027, and is one of the ever-growing number of fast freights which are revolutionizing the railroad industry throughout the country and bringing back the tonnage to legitimate carriers.

R. H. Kindig photograph

"NOBLE AND NUDE AND ANTIQUE"

No devices of "streamlining," no "skyline casings" nor "airflow symmetry" shroud the works of this venerable 2-6-0 as she clatters through the weeds and over the light-weight iron of the Crystal River and San Juan, deep in the Colorado Rockies. There is a forthrightness and functional frankness about its square steam chests, spark arrester, and high domes, however, which, to many, confound the drafts-manship of such notable moderns as Raymond Loewy and Henry Dreyfuss.

MIKE ON THE INLAND

The inland route on the Southern Pacific by way of Bakersfield and Fresno hasn't the scenic advantages of the Coast divisions between Los Angeles and San Fran-cisco but it's just as good for freight and the Espee rolls some enormous fruit blocks over its long, level stretches. Here, under a scorching June sun, is an Espee 2-8-2 with nearly a mile of mixed consist northbound near Merced. The photog-rapher recalls that there were more drifters aboard its gondolas and flat cars than he ever saw on a single train before.

Lucius Beebe photograph

R. H. Kindig photograph

MEMORIAL TO AN EMPIRE BUILDER

The Denver and Salt Lake, perhaps the greatest of all railroading achievements in the United States, which means the world, stands as a memorial to that old lion of the Rockies who, almost single handed financed and engineered the fabled Moffat Route. David H. Moffat envisioned Denver as the railroading center of the country and when other financiers and institutions balked at the fabulous outlay required to span the Colorado Rockies and pierce the Continental Divide with a tunnel six miles long he underwrote the road out of his personal fortune. In the end, after Moffat's death, a series of complex financial setups were necessary to finish the road from Denver to Orested, where it joined the Dotsero cut-off of the Denver and Rio Grande Western, thereby saving substantial time and distance on the Denver–Salt Lake run. To-day the trains of the Rio Grande share trackage rights with the Denver and Salt Lake through the Moffat Tunnel. The photograph shows D & SL No. 303, a ten wheeler emerging from Tunnel 29 and starting over a trestle near Pineville, Colorado, in South Boulder Canyon with Train No. 1.

TITAN OF THE U.P. TRAIL

Three of the driving wheels and the valve gear, with the piston rod disconnected
for delivery deadheaded, of the most powerful freight engine in the world, the
Union Pacific's No. 4001. Built by the American Locomotive Company it is the
first of twenty articulated 4-8-8-4 monsters designed for fast freight service in the
Wasatch Mountains. Its boiler delivers 7000 horsepower, it has a cruising speed of
eighty miles an hour and consumes twelve tons of coal and 15,000 gallons of
water every sixty minutes. Its operating pressure is 300 pounds to the square inch
and the total weight of locomotive and tender is more than 595 tons. 4001 is in
service on the Green River, Wyoming, to Ogden, Utah run, the eastern passage of
which is one of the most exacting freight hauls in the world.

THE NEWSBOY ON ITS ROUNDS

Known as The Newsboy because a large part of its tonnage consists of Canadian newsprint bound for the presses of American dailies, this Central Vermont freight is powered by a rebuilt 2-8-0 and a superpower 2-10-4 as it nears the west end of the St. Albans, Vermont, yards. The road engine of this heavy manifest boasts a Vanderbilt type tender.

William Barham–Ivan Oaks photograph

THE COTTON BELT'S NO. 19

No. 19 on the St. Louis Southwestern rolls into the main at East St. Louis at 4:30 in the afternoon with cars for Texarkana, Shreveport, Fort Worth, Houston and a number of other Texas destinations, most of which will be achieved the next day due to the passenger speed scheduling of this redball merchandise. Sometimes it runs in two sections, and here is the first string of high cars a few miles south of East St. Louis with Mikado No. 770 straining at the drawbars for a fast run southward through the night.

B. & O. BEHEMOTH

Ponderous with power, a Baltimore and Ohio articulated 2-8-8-0 approaches the Pennsylvania crossover near Cambridge, Ohio.

Railroad Photographs

Railroad Photographs

ST. JOHNSBURY AND LAKE CHAMPLAIN

If this 2-8-0 on the head of the St. Johnsbury and Lake Champlain's daily mixed train heading into Swanton, Vermont, seems to resemble the design of Boston and Maine locomotives in general, that is because it was once on the B. & M. power roster. A nice study in old time rural railroading in a New England midst.

Lucius Beebe photograph

MIKE ON THE C. & E. I.

A few railroads, among them the Pennsylvania and the Chicago and Eastern
Illinois, make a practice of equipping their road engines in freight classes with
footboards instead of the more conventional pilot or combination pilot and foot-
board. This C. & E. I. 2-8-2 is drifting through Chicago Heights with a string
of mixed merchandise bound, eventually, for St. Louis. Little of the C. & E. I.'s
power is of strictly modern vintage but it manages very well with what it has.

R. H. Kindig photograph

MINIATURE HOTSHOT

This sightly little U. P. 2-8-0, No. 353, is streaking from Greeley, Colorado, on the main line, to Cloverly on the Pleasant Valley Branch with a lone car of what appears to be redball merchandise tailing a crummy. Here is visual proof that not all the interesting speed shots of railroad are of celebrated varnish hauls or 110-car drags powered by a brace of Mallets.

HIGH CARS EAST

A Reading Mikado, No. 1706, whistles for a grade crossing a few miles out of Elizabeth, New Jersey, on the smoky end of a hundred-odd cars of merchandise out of Pittsburgh and Scranton for the yards at Jersey City.

Lucius Beebe photograph

READING SUPERPOWER

Fresh from the paint shops and with its bright metal gleaming, this Reading super 2-10-2, rebuilt from an earlier Mallet compound is at the head end of eighty-odd cars of mixed consist as it passes through Sinking Spring, Pennsylvania, on the Harrisburg haul. No. 3009 is typical of the graceful and serviceable freight power of the Reading, a road which, more than most eastern roads, keeps its engines sightly and painted at all times.

READY FOR ORDERS

With the head brakeman standing on the cab steps ready to loop up orders, a Peoria and Western 4-8-4 rolls toward Farmington, Illinois. Even in these days of greatly accelerated schedules the carding of the P. & W.'s redballs is considered remarkable by railroad men everywhere.

MERCHANDISE WEST

Through the summer countryside of the Province of Quebec, near Summerlea,
dual-service Pacific No. 2322 of the Canadian Pacific Railway with white flags
on its smokebox wheels a mixed merchandise drag of seventy cars. The enclosed
cab is characteristic of almost all Canadian Pacific locomotives as protection
against the severe winters.

"A MALLET AND A MILLION"

The Union Pacific's M-18 powered by No. 3909 rolls through Weber Canyon, ahead of seventy-two refrigerator and box-cars at thirty miles an hour. There is a pusher behind. The photograph was made on a misty day by Mr. Maxwell with his shutter set at f. 6.3 and a speed of 1/400 of a second.

R. H. Kindig photograph

MIGHTY POWER ON THE ESPEE

This rather terrific looking freight hog is one of the Southern Pacific's 3800 series, a coal-burner articulated with the cab in the conventional position rather than in front as has been the Espee's custom for many years. Built by Lima, it is Class AC-9, 2-8-8-4 with a tractive effort of 124,300 pounds and was designed for use on the Rio Grande Division where this photograph was taken on a westbound extra near Hargis, New Mexico. The Southern Pacific's motive-power officials seldom release action shots showing smoke exhaust, and the photographer was particularly fortunate to catch No. 3800 itself blasting the skies from its stubby stack concealed behind the engine's "skyline casing."

ONE-SPOT IN ACTION

*Upper left:
Paul H. Stringham
photograph*

This rare type of road engine, a 2-8-0, more commonly found in service in yard operations, is No. 1 of the Galesburg and Great Eastern with six loads of company coal from the Little John Mine, near Victoria, Illinois (not to be confused with Colorado's celebrated Little Johnny which financed Denver's Unsinkable Mrs. Brown to the tune of $20,000,000 in gold rush bonanza days). The Galesburg and Great Eastern operates ten miles of road between Victoria and Watega, Illinois, carries freight only and connects with the Burlington.

ROLLING THE EMPTIES

*Lower left:
Railroad
photographs*

No fancy smoke deflectors characterize the Delaware and Hudson's freight power such as that on their passenger engines, but this sturdy 2-8-0 handles seventy-odd empty coal cars through Essex, New York, with a minimum of fuss.

Railroad Photographs

RARE IN EASTERN RAILROADING

Although not infrequent in mountain divisions in the west and along the iron of the Pennsylvania, triple headers like this Canadian Pacific hotshot balling out of Newport, Vermont, aren't common in New England operations. These three light 4-6-0 hogs make up the smoky end of sixty-odd high cars wheeling northward above Lake Memphemagog and make a dramatic camera study as their exhausts slam skyward. H. W. Pontin was the photographer.

BIG POWER ON THE BIG FOUR

Contrary to the usual practice in designing road engines, this New York Central System Mountain type hog is built with footboards instead of the conventional pilot. The chunky proportions characteristic of all Central locomotives required by many narrow clearances along the line's right-of-way, especially in New York State are evidenced in the short stack, cylinders set in close against the frame and the shielding in of the pumps behind the pilot beam instead of hanging them on the accustomed left above the drivers. The engineer is rolling her on the St. Louis run near Terre Haute, Indiana.

OZARK DAWN

With the sun behind the driver's back and the Ozarks reaching ahead, one of the fleet of Frisco Faster Freights heads out on the St. Louis–Tulsa haul on the tail of one of the road's giant coal-burning 4-8-2's, No. 4304. The newest of the Frisco's fast carded freights is the Creole Flash which delivers merchandise in New Orleans the second day out of St. Louis and Kansas City. Fine roadbeds and great reserves of power frequently gone over in the vast company shops at Springfield, Missouri, enable the Frisco to maintain among the fastest freight schedules in the Southwest.

Lucius Beebe photograph

ALTON AND SOUTHERN IN ACTION

The Alton and Southern East St. Louis Outer Belt Line is a connecting road handling thousands of cars of freight daily over its thirty-one miles of operating track. It serves, between its Fox Terminal on the edge of the Mississippi and its northern limit, the Chicago and Alton tracks at Mitchell, the Pennsy, Illinois Central, Mobile and Ohio, the Baltimore and Ohio, Louisville and Nashville and half a score of other roads including the tiny St. Louis and O'Fallon, of which Adolphus Busch III is chairman of the board and whence it derives two full trains of beer daily for distribution to other roads. The Alton and Southern makes a practice of buying a new locomotive a year, No. 15, a powerful Mikado, being one of its latest purchases and shown here at the Pennsylvania crossover near the Madison–St. Clair county line.

pioneer standing. Outstanding are the runs from San Francisco and Los Angeles, 470 miles, and the Arizona Overnight, Los Angeles to Tucson, 502 miles.

The Missouri Pacific operates a large fleet of overnights from St. Louis to Missouri River and Kansas points, also to Memphis and Arkansas points; also out of Kansas City for distances up to 500 miles. Overnights from Houston serve the entire Lower Rio Grande Valley as well as Austin, San Antonio, Dallas and Forth Worth, distances ranging from 250 to 400 miles. Its St. Louis–Pacific Coast schedules have been stepped up so that freight arrives in Los Angeles and Oakland on the fourth evening for early fifth morning delivery; also sixth morning delivery to Portland, Seattle, and Tacoma. Its new redball freight train from St. Louis to Wichita, Kansas gives first morning instead of second morning delivery; also to Joplin, Missouri.

The Chicago, Burlington and Quincy participates in the new schedules cutting a day from Chicago and St. Louis to the West Coast. It has established early first morning delivery from Chicago to Wisconsin, Missouri, and Iowa points; first evening arrival at Billings, Montana, on merchandise from Denver. It has made numerous reductions of from two to twenty hours on various freight trains.

The Texas Pacific makes first morning deliveries up to 450 miles distant. Practically the entire railway between El Paso and New Orleans has one or more daily overnight trains serving important terminals. The Chicago, Rock Island and Pacific's steady development of plant and equipment makes its schedules faster and more dependable than at any time in the road's history. The Chicago, Milwaukee, St. Paul and Pacific, by reason of its new half-million-dollar receiving and transfer station at Galewood, Illinois, permits a twenty-four-hour time-saving on most merchandise handled through Chicago.

The Denver and Rio Grande Western reports that 90 per cent of all its freight trains make schedule. Its overnight Rocket from Denver provides first day delivery to all principal points in Colorado and New Mexico. Its freight trains all are coördinated with the Rio Grande Motor Way Trucks. The Ute, fastest freight train operated by the road, leaves Denver at 5:45 A.M. and arrives in Salt Lake City at 4:30 A.M. next day.

The yield of the great granary of the Middle West and other products in and around the farm belt keep the railroad men on their toes. The Missouri-Kansas-Texas is famous for its Komets. These overnights range between terminals from 328 to 378 miles apart. Its Katy Packer, carrying livestock and perishable meat, makes the run from Fort Worth to Kansas City, 506 miles, in 18 hours, 30 minutes; to St. Louis, 757 miles, in 25 hours, 45 minutes.

The St. Louis–San Francisco operates its renowned fleet of Flashes. It recently added a new one from St. Louis to New Orleans via Boligee, Alabama, and the Southern. Several hours have been cut from the Memphis–St. Louis schedules.

Participating with connections, the Minneapolis and St. Louis joined in cutting a day from Chicago to the Pacific Northwest. Indicative of increased speed, the New York, Chicago and St. Louis reports that the Nickel Plate's average miles per day per freight car has gone up from 64.6 to 67.3. Its overnights speed between Chicago and Cleveland, 336 miles.

The heavy-duty roads have made an exceptional contribution to railroad progress. The Reading made history by establishing overnight service on coal from Pennsylvania anthracite fields to tidewater. The Duluth, Missabe and Iron Range has one main job, moving ore to the head of the lakes. It has continuously been improving its equipment to do that job better. The Bessemer and Lake Erie has greatly expanded its equipment, and its heavy tonnage operations are being conducted with increasing efficiency. The Chicago and Illinois Midland, one of the largest coal-originating carriers, is also paying attention to general business, including perishables.

The flow of traffic between New York and Buffalo gets a wealth of attention from the railroads. The Delaware, Lackawanna and Western has as its leader the New York–Buffalo overnight. The Westbound Overnight handles forty-five to fifty carloads and runs the 395 miles in 11 hours, 30 minutes. The Lehigh Valley between the same points but over a longer route averages 35 m.p.h. for its run of 446 miles. The Erie, between Jersey City and Buffalo maintains approximately the same speed. The Erie has been engaged on an immense modernization freight program, so much so, that it has practically rebuilt or replaced the bulk of its cars.

Running time on Delaware and Hudson manifest trains is down, and train loads are up. The D. & H. provides four daily trains between the Canadian border and the Wilkes-Barre and Binghamton gateways. The New York Central has fast overnights speeding between all its important terminals. Its trains between New York and Buffalo, 429 miles, operate on a schedule of 10 hours 50 minutes. Its East St. Louis to New York run, 1156 miles, is scheduled at 47 hours 30 minutes.

The Pennsylvania operates numerous fast freights. It has six speedsters operating between the New York–Philadelphia–Baltimore and Pittsburgh areas. It shares heavily in transcontinental freight. Two fast freight trains run daily between Enola and East St. Louis; two from Enola to Chicago, three from Chicago to Enola. As speed examples, consider the several Pennsylvania trains daily between Potomac Yard and Jersey City. Distance, 229 miles. Time, seven hours.

The Illinois Central's overnights number six and operate over distances between 313 and 527 miles. Speed economies compared to former schedules range from one hour to a complete business day.

Canadian National's overnight service between Montreal and Toronto operates in two sections, sometimes three, every night. Wartime traffic has brought big problems, but the pre-war schedules are being steadfastly maintained.

The Baltimore and Ohio has shared in schedule reductions necessary to cut a full day on perishable freight from Florida to New York and New England. The longest B. & O. overnight runs are between Jersey City and Pittsburgh, 525 miles. The average overall speed is 41.3 m.p.h. Running time is 12 hours 45 minutes. Most of the B. & O. less-than-carload schedules have been reduced by twenty-four hours.

Speaking of New England, the Central Vermont, the Boston and Maine–Maine Central, and the New York, New Haven and Hartford, all have done their bit in speeding up freight delivery. The Central Vermont's Rocket provides overnight service to Vermont points from Boston and southern New England. The Newsboy, so named because it handles newsprint from Quebec to New England, has been speeded up. The Maine

Bullet, operated by the B. & M. in connection with the New Haven, gives overnight service on merchandise from Portland, Dover, New Hampshire, and Lowell, Massachusetts, to New York. The B. & M. provides overnight service from Boston and other terminals throughout New England in connection with the Maine Central, New Haven, Central Vermont, and the Rutland.

Jumping west again, one may take an admiring glance at Atchison, Topeka and Sante Fe. Twenty-four hours have been chopped off deliveries on carload and less-than-carload freight from Chicago, St. Louis and Missouri points to destinations in California; likewise on less-than-carload traffic Chicago to El Paso. Merchandise originating at Chicago has second morning delivery at points as far west as Amarillo and Albuquerque. Outstanding among on-time records is that of the Green Fruit Express, California to the East: 99.8 per cent on time for an entire year! The Sante Fe potato specials from growing areas in Missouri are operated 450 miles to give 5:00 A.M. first morning delivery at the Chicago produce terminal. No. 39, Chicago to Kansas City, 449 miles, has an on-time record of 97 per cent. Running time, 13 hours 30 minutes. This fast freight started with a consist of twenty-six cars. Now it runs fifty cars nightly. The Sante Fe is, as is detailed elsewhere, a pioneer in using Diesel locomotives in regular mainline freight operation.

The Chicago and Northwestern's fleet of mainline freights between Chicago, Milwaukee, and terminal and interchange points in the Middle West and Northwest have been cutting time. Between Chicago and Council Bluffs the maximum permitted speed for freight trains has been pushed up from 50 to 60 miles per hour.

On the Great Northern, twenty hours have been lopped off Train 401, Minneapolis to Seattle. Various overnighters out of Minneapolis are making faster runs. The Minneapolis, St. Paul and Sault Ste. Marie (Soo to its friends) has improved service to Chicago by twelve hours. The Chicago Great Western participates in various schedules from Chicago to the far West, helping to shorten the overland run by a full day. Its perishable trains to Chicago from St. Paul and Minneapolis, also from Omaha, Des Moines, and St. Joseph, are high-speed runs. Some give 3:00 A.M. arrival at the Chicago produce markets.

A notable nighthawk on the schedules of the Pere Marquette, running through the dense industrial regions of the Great Lakes is the Over-nighter, flagship of the P. M.'s fleet of fast freights between Detroit and Chicago. A train of several years' standing, it has become an institution among shippers both of heavy durables and less-than-carload lots, leaving Detroit's Boat Yard as Train No. 41 at 5:45 in the afternoon and arriving in Chicago at 3:00 the next morning with overnight delivery between shipping sources at both industrial capitals. The northbound section leaves Chicago as No. 40 at 7:00 P.M. and reaches Detroit at 5:30 A.M. The Overnighter is customarily powered with a heavy-service Berkshire locomotive and hauls from thirty-five to forty cars.

Via the Overnighter it is possible to leave cargo at the Detroit terminal freight house as late as four in the afternoon for early morning delivery in Chicago. Make-up for No. 41 derives from four principal revenue sources: the National Carloading Company at Detroit, the P. M.'s own freight collection service, carload freight of eastern Canadian sources traveling over Canadian Pacific and ferried across from Windsor, Ontario, and from carloads from Detroit manufactories. A couple of carloads of automobile parts are customarily picked up at Lansing, Michigan, and as many as fifteen may be set out and as many picked up at Grand Rapids. There are set-outs at Rockwell Street in Chicago and end of run is at Clearing Yard.

Another fast freight run over the Pere Marquette is known as DC 1 (Detroit-Chicago No. 1) leaving Detroit at 3:30 in the morning and arriving at Chicago twenty-four and three quarters hours later. On both of these trains the crew, motive-power, and way car are changed when the consist is rebuilt at Grand Rapids.

Few indeed, if any, are the roads which have not shared in the general speeding up of freight movement. No reviewer should fail to mention the Wabash with its fast overnight service between its principal terminals. It provides next day delivery between St. Louis and Des Moines, 340 miles, and between East St. Louis and Detroit, 488 miles. The Pere Marquette maintains high speed overnight freight service between Chicago and Detroit. The Chesapeake and Ohio's overnight meat and livestock trains from Chicago give not later than 4:30 A.M. placement at

Cincinnati. The Chicago and Eastern Illinois freight schedules have been so adjusted to movements with other lines that practically through service is maintained in all directions, without terminal or interchange delays. The Western Maryland has improved its schedule by several hours, mainly through the addition of much new power. The Norfolk and Western is engaged in a $5,000,000 expansion program for improved terminal facilities at Roanoke. Freight handling will be greatly speeded thereby.

And so it has been going and continues to go. Better and better facilities, faster and faster deliveries! All in all, there never has been a period when the freight picture of the railroads looked as bright. By the time 1950 rolls around, the story which may be written about progress in railroad freight service will dwarf any up to date. Modern freight transportation is as different from what it was a bare generation ago as the horse and buggy days are different from to-day. At the rate freight speed is climbing and service to shippers is expanding, 1950 should have a bright tale to tell.

Lucius Beebe photograph

Lucius Beebe photograph

2
The Diesel Dream

FEW chapters in history illustrate the inborn American desire to find new and better ways of doing the day's work than the development of Diesel motive-power on United States railroads. The story serves also to highlight other useful characteristics of the men who have guided the progress of the nation's rail system. It is an excellent case example of how widely the railroads tap the skills of other industries in order to give better public service.

Many persons believe that Diesel motive-power grew out of the automotive industry, that it suddenly came into existence in 1933 when the Pioneer Zephyr of the Burlington Railroad, the world's first Diesel-powered mainline passenger train, quickly followed by the Union Pacific's City of Portland streaked their first silver and yellow paths on exhibition tours about the country. The movement, however, goes much further back than that. Those epoch-making first appearances of Diesel motive-power on the mainlines might be likened only to graduation from preparatory school. Likewise, the idea that the Diesel locomotive was the product of automotive engineers is equally far from the truth. It is quite true that automotive engineers contributed importantly to the development of the Diesel locomotive as it appears on the railroads to-day, but the men who brought together all the various skills involved into the product that finally was able to take its place with other forms of motive-power were men who grew up in the engineering or operating departments of railroads or who had had long experience in the design and manufacture of rail power. It is extremely difficult also to mark the line where original work of the executives and employes of the companies which manufacture Diesel locomotives can be separated from the suggestions that came from railroad management and employes. If ever there was a case of evolution, as opposed to the term invention, the development of the Diesel locomotive is it. However, the fact remains that the guiding genius, the coördinator who finally brought the thinking of all the contributing skills into the present rapidly growing new form of motive-power was a railroad man, so much of a railroad man that he started his career as a fireman on the Southern Pacific in California. Subsequently, he was a boomer engineer, working his way behind the throttles of freight and passenger trains on railroads from coast to coast. He was once a minor road official of the Florida East Coast Railway. No one can tell to what degree this experience was responsible for his ultimate accomplishment, but certainly he gained a knowledge of the motive-power problems of the railroads that was a powerful factor. And, certainly, the established fact is that it was a railroad man who finally put Diesel on the mainlines. This man is Harold L. Hamilton, President of Electro-Motive Corporation, subsidiary of General Motors at LaGrange, Illinois.

The real root of the adaptation of Diesel power to rails lies in the relative thermal efficiencies of various prime movers. From the very moment that the gasoline engine first began to be successful on the highways some forty years ago, progressive railroad engineers began thinking about whether there would be any gain in the adaptation of the internal-combustion engine to railroad propulsion. The Diesel engine did not come into these early calculations to any extent, although it is true that the Diesel was invented in 1897 by Rudolph Diesel, an Austrian, at approximately the same time that the gasoline engine was appearing in the horseless carriage. The interest of railroad mechanical engineers in the internal-combustion engine was centered in its higher thermal efficiency than steam engines. Popularly stated, thermal efficiency is a measure of an engine's ability to put to use the potential energy in a given amount of fuel. The ordinary steam engine of only a few years ago had a thermal efficiency of from 5 to 8 per cent, a ratio that has been considerably stepped up of late. The gasoline engine has from 20 to 25 per cent and the Diesel engine from 33 to 38 per cent. Modern steam turbines are said to get as high as 20 to 25 per cent efficiency. The steam turbine, as yet, has not been successfully adapted to railroad propulsion, but engineers long have been working on this idea.

The thought, then, of the dreamers in the railroad motive-power field was that if they could get an engine that would convert one-fourth to one-third of the fuel's potential energy into work instead of only about one-twentieth to one-tenth, as then was being accomplished with steam locomotives, an important contribution to rail progress would be made. There was the added advantage that the fuel burned by internal-combustion engines was less bulky than the coal and oil burned by steam locomotives. Not only would the problem of transporting the fuel with the locomotive be lessened, but also it would be less expensive to transmit the fuel to and store it at fueling points. Granted that there are highly valuable advertising and publicity values in the brightly colored Diesel passenger trains now flashing about the country, it was hard-headed engineering and commercial considerations such as these that led the railroads into exploration and final utilization of the internal-combustion engine.

The usual process of introduction of a striking innovation on the railroads was reversed in the case of the internal-combustion engine. Ordinarily, spectacular railroading innovations burst into public view upon the mainlines, in crack passenger trains, in the show-window, so to speak. But in this case the innovation was put to work on the lowly branch line, and it was many years before it was allowed to take a place with the lordly monarchs of the double-tracked, rock-ballasted, block signal protected right-of-way.

The earliest recorded worth-while application of the internal-combustion engine to the job of propelling a standard railroad car came in 1905 when the first rail motor-car was built by the Union Pacific Railroad. This was the forerunner of the McKeen Motor Car industry fostered by the late E. H. Harriman. The car was thirty-one feet long and was propelled by a 100-horsepower gasoline engine with direct, mechanical drive.

Practically coincident with this development, the General Electric Company had begun work in Schenectady, New York, on a gasoline motor-car with electric drive for the Delaware and Hudson Railway Company. The records indicate that work was started on this car late in 1904 but it was not brought out until February 1, 1906, giving the McKeen car a few months' leeway as the first actually to appear on the rails.

The McKeen Company between 1905 and American entrance into the first World War built 155 cars, some of which still are operating. Sixteen were known to be still in service in 1941 on the Union Pacific. Esthetically they are no paradigms of beauty.

While General Electric put a few units in service between 1906 and 1910, it did not go into real production on the gas-electric rail car until 1910. Between then and 1917 when the activity was switched to war work, approximately ninety of these cars went into service. They went into branch-line service, being unsuited, in speed and carrying ability, for the mainlines.

Neither company revived its activity after the first World War. The experience during this early period, however, had served to demonstrate the practicability of one phase of design which since has proved vital in the evolution of the modern Diesel locomotive. This was that directly geared mechanical transmission had limitations which electric transmission could far surpass. There were very definite limits as to the strains of starting heavy weights which gears could withstand. But the power of an electric motor remains practically constant at any speed. It can start pulling the heavy weight of a railroad car with all its force without strain.

Engineers clung to the dream of gear drive for the natural reason that it would be far cheaper to construct and instal than generators and motors with the necessary control apparatus. During the time that General Electric and McKeen were developing and making their cars, other attempts to put gear-driven cars on the rails were made, chiefly by the early motor-truck manufacturers. In fact, there is some evidence that a number of these companies went bankrupt trying to get on the railroads. The lure of profits in shuttling thousands of fast-moving flanged wheeled buses and trucks along on rails was bright, but success failed to materialize.

Rail-car development lay dormant between the early days of the first World War and 1922, when it was due for a sudden and historically important revival. The story of Harold L. Hamilton comes back in at this point. Hamilton had left the railroads and, of all things, became an automobile and truck salesman. He had climbed in one of the early automotive organizations, still in existence, to the post of Western Sales Manager with headquarters at Denver. He had watched the abortive attempts of the motor companies to put buses and trucks on the rails. He was familiar

R. H. Kindig photograph

THIS TRAIN SOLD THE BILL OF GOODS

Electro-Motive sold the Atchison, Topeka and Santa Fe its first Diesel-electric freight units on the strength of this demonstration engine, General Motors No. 103. The greatest horsepower producers in the vast Santa Fe power roster are the monster Texas type steam locomotives of the 5001 Class built by Baldwin for heavy freight service. They weigh 905,000 pounds as against 924,000 pounds for a four-unit Diesel-electric unit and cost approximately a third as much. Furthermore steam has a sentimental appeal to all railroaders and, in fact, to almost everyone not actively engaged in the designing, building, and merchandising of Diesel-electric power. With the aid of G. M. 103, shown here with forty-two cars and a dynamometer unit (directly behind the engine) on a Denver and Rio Grande Western freight climbing the east approach to the Moffat Tunnel in the Colorado Rockies, the General Motors salesmen had no difficulty in selling the Santa Fe executives their bill of goods. The Diesel's chief selling point was its ability to travel with a 5000-ton paying load five hundred miles without pause for servicing, inspection, or for refueling.

TRANSITION ON THE Q

The exposition flyer, on the Chicago–San Francisco run, passes over the iron of the Burlington, the Rio Grande, and Western Pacific. Here it is shown fifty miles east of Denver powered by the Burlington's 4000-horsepower Diesel-electric unit No. 9912 while its consist includes standard-weight coaches, Pullmans, and mail cars as well as light-weight streamlined cars from the Burlington's increasing fleet of these gleaming units.

COMPANION TO THE DIXIELAND

The Dixie Flagler is a companion train on the Chicago and Eastern Illinois' sailing list with the Dixieland and shares the Chicago and Midwest stream-lined chair car service to Florida with the Illinois Central's City of Miami and the Pennsylvania's flashing South Wind. Its smartly appointed lounges and res-taurant cars are annually populated with vacationists anxious to secure luxury service and appointments at the lowest available fares, and it leaves Miami and Chicago every third day, stopping en route at Nashville, Chattanooga, Atlanta, and Jacksonville and covering its final divisions behind the single-unit Florida East Coast Diesel-electric engine which the photographer caught as it was rolling at a smooth seventy near Lake Worth in deepest Florida.

VERSATILE AND SIGHTLY

The general adaptability of the Texas and Pacific Railroad's Pacific type power, which is designed either for passenger or light freight over the level Texas prairies, is illustrated as this 4-6-2 rolls out of Roanoke ahead of a tidy cut of hot freight. T. & P. power and rolling stock are notoriously favorites with photographers and train lovers in general because of their beauty of design and state of maintenance. Number plates, valve gear and rod assemblies, lamps, and cylinder heads are invariably gleaming in the best railroading tradition.

THE BLUEBONNET

As it is shown here this modest five-car Missouri–Kansas–Texas overnight is setting out at dusk from Fort Worth. By the time it reaches St. Louis the next morning on the iron of the Frisco, it will have grown two or even three times its present length. The power is a Katy Pacific of mature years but it will require a new and powerful Frisco Mountain type to haul its consist over the Ozarks.

VINTAGE SPRINTER

This aged but spry Atlantic type is in commuting service on the Chicago and North Western and is shown racing along at a good seventy near Lake Forest. Although almost a collector's item, those high drivers can wheel a light train of coaches at a speed the most up-to-the-minute Diesel greyhound might envy.

"DIVIDES THE DESERT AND THE SOWN"

Somewhere between Indio and Palm Springs, California, this Southern Pacific 4-8-2, No. 3655, is entering a new block with only the dust of the desert blown up beneath the trucks of its following cars to show that it is moving at all. Seldom, except on stiff grades or when the fireboy is sanding his flues, do Espee oil burners show the rolling smoke exhaust so dear to railroad photographers.

Lucius Beebe photograph

"MADE UP OF WHEELS, THE NEW MECHANIC BIRTH"

Pride of the Gulf, Mobile and Ohio Railroad Company are Trains No. 15 and 16, the Gulf Coast Rebel, a silver and crimson-lacquered Diesel-electric streamliner which operates between East St. Louis and Mobile on a schedule of no breathtaking acceleration, but satisfactory to the requirements of the run. Its consist includes standard Pullman accommodations with double bedrooms and drawing-rooms, luxury coaches, and lunch and diner service. Here, with a carload of strawberries included for head-end revenue, it greets a summer's dawn on its northbound haul through the Illinois meadows a half score of miles south of East St. Louis.

A CENTURY OF THE PONY EXPRESS

Heading out of Denver for Kansas City behind Diesel-electric units 9-M-1 and 9-M-2 with a total of 4000 horsepower is the Union Pacific's Train No. 38, the Pony Express with nine cars of mail and passengers. The ultra-modernity of its power units integrated with the historic symbolism of the train's name form an interesting commentary on modern communications.

R. H. Kindig photograph

THE MERCHANT'S LIMITED

Powered by one of the Shoreliner Class of Hudsons, No. 1402, the New York, New Haven and Hartford's celebrated Merchant's Limited tops Sharon Hill, the ruling grade on the Boston–New York run. The photograph was taken at dusk by H. W. Pontin, and the engine driver is seen giving him a hand as he rolls across the camera's finder. The Merchant's is an extra-fare all-Pullman train, the only one on the line since the Yankee Clipper began carrying coach passengers a few months ago.

ALONG THE LEHIGH VALLEY

Three railroads, the Lehigh Valley, the Erie, and the Lackawanna—the last two feeding their traffic to the Nickel Plate at Buffalo—maintain slower and less elaborate trains on the New York–Chicago run than do the more important New York Central and Pennsylvania and hence are allowed to charge a lower or differential fare. The Lehigh has streamlined and reconditioned some of its locomotives and rolling stock, painting them a flashing red with gold trim, and this is the John Wilkes passing West Dunellen, New Jersey. In Manhattan the Lehigh shares the facilities of the Pennsylvania Terminal. Note the novel smoke deflector of the locomotive, the countersunk headlight and the curved handrails, as well as the neatly manicured roadbed.

Lucius Beebe photograph

VANISHING RACE

Camelbacks, like this Central Railroad of New Jersey ten-wheeler, are fast disappearing from the mainlines of the land and being relegated to suburban service and yard operations. Once a numerous race, they populated the iron of the Central of New Jersey, the Reading, and the Long Island, but government regulations ruled that the separation of fireman and engineer, one behind the firebox and the other astride the boiler was unsafe practice and no more camelbacks are being built. This one is pulling a commuters' local near Cranford, New Jersey.

Lucius Beebe photograph

STEAM, STREAMLINING, AND SEACOAST

Loafing along at a casual and exquisite forty miles an hour near Santa Barbara, California, the Southern Pacific's famed Daylight poses for its photograph against the desolate mountains that skirt the Pacific Ocean for hundreds of miles. Characteristic of the Espee's orange and silver painted giant Northern type engines is the smoke and steam lifter developed by General Superintendent of Motive Power George McCormick and Mechanical Engineer F. E. Russel, with details worked out at the Lima Locomotive Works, builders of the road's Daylight class locomotives. This deflector and the "skyline casing" which encloses sand domes and other operating fixtures runs the length of the boiler lagging and has been so sightly and successful that the Espee is adapting it to many older locomotives of both freight and passenger classifications in process of reconditioning.

General Motors photograph

"HIS HEART A SPINNING COIL,
HIS JUICES BURNING OIL—"

There is no romance about the ordered precision of a Diesel-electric power-plant, but there is serenity, economy of motion, and vast implications of titanic strength. When in full operation hardly a moving part meets the eye, but the very absence of accustomed motion serves as a dramatic understatement of speed and power and controlled forces. This is the engine room of an 1800-horsepower passenger locomotive unit looking toward the rear from the door to the driver's cab.

Lucius Beebe photograph

WONDER AND GLORY OF THE MOPAC

is the road's streamline Diesel-electric powered Eagle on the St. Louis–Kansas City–Omaha daily run, here shown rolling proudly at better than seventy a few miles west of Tower Grove, Missouri. Built by the American Car and Foundry Company and powered by the Electro-Motive Corporation, each of the two six-car Eagle units consists of a mail-storage car, a baggage-mail, one coach, one de luxe coach, one diner-lounge, and a parlor-observation car. The train was styled by Raymond Loewy who also designed the Pennsylvania's Broadway Limited, and combines the most luxurious appointments of day train travel with the most modern features of motive-power and operation.

THUNDER ON THE HUDSON

Most of the locomotives assigned during the nineties to the run of the Central's famed Empire State Express bore the train name in flowing golden script on the tender. No. 862 on the Central's power roster was evidently taken from some other run when this photograph was made near Poughkeepsie during the middle nineties and carried only the initials of the New York Central and Hudson River. Engineer Charles Hogan hung up the all-time speed record at the throttle of No. 999 when he covered a measured mile with the Empire State between Syracuse and Buffalo in May, 1893 at 112.5 miles an hour. Mortal man had never traveled faster and, except in the air, he doesn't do it very frequently to-day. On the speedway west of La Junta the Santa Fe's streamliners sometime hit 110 and 115 but it isn't a comfortable speed either for train crew or passengers. The Empire State is now, like the Central's Mercury and Twentieth Century Limited, a streamliner with up-to-the-minute appointments of luxury.

SLEEK AND SILVER TRIMMED

The Louisville and Nashville's Dixieland, No. 91, southbound behind a meticulously groomed Pacific near East St. Louis, Illinois.

William Barham–Ivan Oaks photograph

DIESEL ON THE ALTON

Among the leading and pioneer purchasers of Diesel-electric power in the east were the Alton and Baltimore and Ohio railroads. Here is the Alton's Abraham Lincoln on the St. Louis–Chicago run, northbound, near Alton, Illinois. Running in competition with the Wabash's Banner Blue and Blue Bird, the C. & E. I.'s St. Louis Zipper and the Illinois Central's Daylight and Green Diamond, the stream-lined Abraham Lincoln includes in its consist reclining seat chair cars, drawing-room parlor cars, a forty-seat dining-room–tavern car, buffet-lounge, observation, and head-end revenue cars. Note the unusual type of skeleton semaphore in the speed photograph.

SEABOARD AT SUNSET

The Seaboard Railway's all-coach flyer on the New York–Miami run, the Silver
Meteor, which rolls from Manhattan's Pennsylvania Station to its Florida terminal daily during the winter season in a flat twenty-five hours, is shown streaking across the Florida meadows on the last lap of its southbound run near Fort
Lauderdale of a late winter afternoon.

J. W. Maxwell photograph

ERA'S END

With a mixed consist, and to the grief of narrow-gage sentimentalists and enthusiasts, Colorado and Southern's (a Burlington subsidiary) three locomotives, Nos. 70, 71, and 69, are making the last run from Black Hawk to Denver on the short line which served such romantic cities of the frontier legend as Central City, Silver Plume, and Georgetown. Central City, which still celebrates its fragrant past with an annual drama festival and frontier fiesta is famed for its Eureka Street, Teller House and Opera, its Gregory's Gulch, Glory Hole, Boston Mine, and the memories of H. A. W. (Silver Dollar) Tabor, Horace Greeley, and General Grant. It was in these storied hills that Greeley was inspired to his celebrated line: "Go west, young man."

with the General Electric development. The notion that the internal combustion engine, with its higher thermal efficiency, could do a better job for the railroads kept bobbing up in his mind. He and an associate in motor-truck selling talked about it frequently. The idea grew until Hamilton, out of his own pocket, hired a draftsman to work part time, nights, in a Denver hotel room with him and his friend. They finally produced a set of drawings embodying Hamilton's ideas on what a successful gas-electric rail car should be. In 1922 he threw up his job as a truck salesman and for months, living on savings, rang doorbells in financial centers until finally he obtained sufficient capital to build his first car. He farmed out the job, of course, to another builder, having no factory of his own. The car was completed in 1923 and sent on demonstration runs. It was bought almost immediately. That financed the construction of another, and the Electro-Motive Company headed by the once fireman on the S.P. was on its way. In the ensuing seven years Electro-Motive sent out more than five hundred rail cars. Practically all of them still are in operation upon branch lines to this day.

The engineering and manufacturing organization gathered together by Hamilton amassed a tremendous fund of information upon application of the internal combustion engine in the design and construction of these rail cars. They progressed to the point where, in 1929, they powered a three-car train, which some authorities regard as the legitimate ancestor of the streamlined trains which began to appear in 1934.

This early gasoline-electric train was the Blue Bird of the Chicago and Great Western. It operated, for a few months, between Minneapolis and Rochester, Minnesota, being designed largely to serve traffic to and from the Mayo Brothers' Clinic. This train served chiefly to demonstrate that from both mechanical and economic standpoints the gasoline engine in bigger sizes and higher horsepowers was not the ideal solution of how to get the internal combustion engine out on the mainlines. Limitations both as to durability and economy cropped out in these higher horsepowers.

Hamilton and his organization, as well as railroad mechanical engineers, had been thoughtfully considering Diesel engines for several years. Actually the Diesel locomotive already was on the rails—in switching service—and there had been a dismally unsuccessful attempt to put a

5000-horsepower Diesel mainline locomotive in service on the Canadian National Railroad. The American development had started with a 300-horsepower Diesel-electric switching locomotive developed jointly by American Locomotive Company, General Electric, and Ingersoll-Rand in 1924. A few more switchers had been built, primarily to meet the demand of railroads facing anti-smoke ordinances in several cities. No attempt was made to push the Diesel switcher for general adoption.

The chief bar to adoption of Diesel engines on mainline work was that those with enough horsepower to do mainline work were enormous in size and weight. The best available American Diesel engine at that time weighed approximately one hundred pounds per horsepower—as compared with five or six pounds per horsepower for a good gasoline engine—and it was difficult to get them into a one-story building, let alone within the necessary limits of a railroad car.

Once again, development work going on elsewhere gravitated to the slowly forming conception of a Diesel mainline locomotive. Charles F. Kettering, General Motors Research Chief, had been working, aided by the engineers of the Winton Engine Company at Cleveland, on reduction in the size and weight of Diesels. The thought was that some day Diesels might be needed in automotive products. Winton already was manufacturing gasoline engines for Electro-Motive rail cars and was one of the leading American manufacturers of Diesel. In 1930, General Motors acquired both Winton and Electro-Motive with the idea of carrying on wider and more practical Diesel development. Hamilton remained at the head of the rail-car business which now became Electro-Motive Corporation and retained the original organization. The Winton organization also was kept intact.

The depression had practically dried up the market for rail cars. This left the Electro-Motive organization free to wander farther afield in development. Kettering and the Winton engineers were plugging away on sweating down the Diesel, and early in 1933 they came out with the first Diesel that looked really practicable for railroad use. It was a two-cycle engine which was one-fourth the size and one-fifth the weight of the best high horsepower Diesels available hitherto.

Two railroads immediately were interested, the Burlington and the

Union Pacific. Both placed orders with Electro-Motive to power streamlined trains with a 600-horsepower model of this new, smaller engine. The Burlington came out first with its Pioneer Zephyr built by the Edwin G. Budd Company, power-plant supplied by Electro-Motive, and the Union Pacific City of Portland, built by Pullman Standard Car Company with the same arrangement of power-plant, was on the rails approximately five months later. The Union Pacific hit the rails first, however, with a streamlined train, the City of Salina, built by Pullman and powered by a Winton distillate engine, preceding the Zephyr by a month.

Here was a Diesel engine at last, small enough and light enough to fit railroad-car limits, yet powerful enough to propel mainline passenger trains at sustained average speeds higher than had been attained in any regular schedules before. The fundamental problems of car construction and electric transmission had been worked out in the rail-car business. The stage was set for the first time for a real attack on the job of putting internal combustion engines on the mainlines. All the materials and the know-how were available, and progressive railroad management immediately supplied the other necessary factor, the demand. There followed a rapid development period in which it is difficult to keep events in proper chronological order.

The first few Diesel trains were articulated, that is, the cars were permanently joined together. It did not take long to demonstrate that for any other service than short-day runs this did not permit proper flexibility. The whole train had to be tied up if repairs were necessary on one car. If anything were wrong with the power car it was impossible to replace it at once with another. The demand for a separate Diesel mainline locomotive came promptly on the heels of the success of the articulated trains. Some railroads wanted to haul regular Pullman and day-coach equipment.

The Santa Fe and the Baltimore and Ohio were the first roads urgently to request Electro-Motive to develop independent Diesel locomotives for mainline service. Electro-Motive developed a 3600-horsepower experimental locomotive in 1934-35 and sent it on trial runs on several eastern and western railroads. The locomotive demonstrated amazing ability to maintain sustained high speeds and to make time by quick acceleration and freedom from frequent service stops. The Baltimore and Ohio placed an order for an 1800-horsepower locomotive and the Santa Fe for a 3600-horsepower locomotive. The first B. & O. locomotive went into service on the Royal Blue between Newark and Washington, later being transferred to the Abraham Lincoln of the Alton between St. Louis and Chicago.

It remained for the Santa Fe Railway to take the lead in demonstrating the most startling possibilities in the new locomotive by the inauguration of the Super Chief, on May 12, 1936, with a separate 3600-horsepower Diesel locomotive and specially painted standard-weight Pullman cars, on a 39¾-hour schedule between Los Angeles and Chicago. The Santa Fe cut ten hours off the previous fastest service on this run with the Super Chief.

Three days after the inauguration of the Super Chief the Chicago and North Western and Union Pacific put the first City of Los Angeles, a light-weight Pullman train, in service between Chicago and Los Angeles on a rival 39¾-hour schedule. Later the Super Chief was replaced by two trains of modern light-weight streamlined cars propelled by a stream-lined Diesel 3600-horsepower locomotive. The City of Los Angeles was ultimately replaced by two ultra modern seventeen-car trains including three-unit 6000-horsepower Diesel locomotives. Transcontinental service boomed. The City of Portland of the Chicago and North Western and Union Pacific already was operating between Chicago and Portland, and it was put on a 39¾-hour schedule. The Chicago and North Western, Union Pacific, and Southern Pacific City of San Francisco was born with the same fast schedule. Each of these trains later were replaced with longer, more luxurious equipment, and more powerful locomotives.

One other significant event during this period of 1935-36 served to drive home conviction among railroad men that the Diesel locomotive was here to stay on long-distance, de luxe, fast-schedule service. The 1025-mile stretch between Denver and Chicago represented in the minds of enterprising passenger traffic executives a lucrative field for improved service. The fastest rail connection between these two important travel centers was twenty-five hours. Both the Burlington and the Chicago and North Western–Union Pacific routes appeared to be wide open with opportunity. The Burlington won the race to put the first Diesel trains in service on this route by switching two of its original small Diesel day-coach trains, the Pioneer and the Mark Twain Zephyrs to this route on a sixteen-hour schedule on May 31, 1936. The C. & N. W.–U. P. combination, however, came along on June 18, 1936, with the first overnight sleeper service, the two City of Denver trains on the same sixteen-hour schedule. On November 7th of the same year the Burlington replaced the day-coach trains with the new sleeper Denver Zephyrs, and Denver thus was handed probably the finest overnight, fast-train service of any city of its size in the world. The Diesel locomotive buckled into the 65-mile-an-hour average schedules for 1025 miles with uninterrupted success.

Meanwhile, the development of light-weight, rapid-schedule, de luxe, low-fare day-coach Diesel service had been coincidental with the success of the longer runs. The Burlington was having conspicuous success with Diesel power on the Twin City Zephyrs on the 882-mile a day round trip runs between Chicago and St. Paul–Minneapolis, at an average speed between St. Paul and Chicago of 71 miles an hour. The Flying Yankee of the Boston and Maine and Maine Central between Boston, Portland, and Bangor, The Comet of the New Haven between Boston and Providence, The Rebels of the Gulf Mobile and Northern between New Orleans and Jackson, Tennessee, and the Green Diamond of the Illinois Central between Chicago and St. Louis also were successes from the operating viewpoint, not to mention profit and prestige. The Rock Island burst into the Diesel column with six fast coach trains at once.

It is not the intention in this consideration of the rise of Diesel motive-power to attempt to cover in detail or chronologically the establishment of all the trains now operating in the country. The intent has been to show how the Diesel locomotive gradually has been developed by the manufacturers and the railroads themselves to fit into the various classes of service. So far we have seen the Diesel locomotive applied to long-distance sleeper service and medium and relatively short de luxe coach runs. There were other fields in which Diesel had yet to win its spurs.

For instance, practical railroad men ran into a large question mark when they considered whether Diesel was applicable to the hauling of long, standard-weight Pullman trains, or whether this type of locomotive could haul freight. Many factors other than merely whether the locomotive can get a given number of passengers from here to there in a certain time enter into such problems. Repair and operating costs were among the other considerations of greatest importance. So, when the Baltimore and Ohio in 1937 applied 3600-horsepower Diesel locomotives to its Capitol Limited on the 750-mile daily run between Chicago and Washington over the tough grades of the Alleghenies as well as the relatively level run across the plains of Ohio and Indiana, watchful eyes were focused. The new locomotives handled the sixteen-hour schedule with from nine to as many as fourteen standard Pullman cars with such a record for continuity of service and economy of operation and maintenance that their availability for this type of service was well on the way toward being proved. When the Seaboard put 6000-horsepower, three-unit Diesels on its Orange Blossom Specials between Washington and Miami at the start of the 1938-39 Florida winter season and they maintained a shortened schedule, hauling the standard Pullman fourteen-car train successfully, the evidence became more convincing. A number of other successes in the heavy-train field finally have cemented the general acceptance of Diesel as being suitable for this service. Among these instances has been the application of 6000-horsepower Diesels by the Atlantic Coast Line to its crack standard Pullman trains between Washington and Florida, the combination train the Exposition Flyer of the Burlington between Chicago and Denver, and the double duty to which the Chicago and North Western assigned the 4000-horsepower Diesels of its famous 400 between Minneapolis–St. Paul and Chicago. The two locomotives assigned to the 400 each pull one of the de luxe 400's during daylight hours on a one-way trip. At night they are assigned to the slower schedule for a one-way trip hauling the sixteen- to eighteen-car standard Pullman Northwestern Limited between the same terminals. The two locomotives in this double, over 800-mile-a-day duty operated for more than one year without missing a trip. One of the locomotives on the Capitol Limited hung up a record of 367 days of continuous operation before it had to miss a trip for shop repairs of an important nature.

While the demand upon the motive-power was similar to that in the de luxe sleeper service, another development during 1938 and 1939 was significant in the march of Diesel to its place as accepted mainline motive-power.

The Santa Fe Railroad, which rapidly was becoming one of the greatest of the pioneers in the application of the new power, on February 20, 1938, inaugurated its El Capitans. These are de luxe, extra fare coach trains operating between Chicago and Los Angeles on the same 39¾-hour schedule as the Super Chief and the City of Los Angeles. They were such a success that the problem ever since has been one of how to add enough cars and motive-power for the increased traffic within economic and operating limits. The Seaboard had similar success with its Silver Meteor, New York–Miami coach train, a year later, and a number of other trains such as the Illinois Central City of Miami between Chicago and Miami and the Southern's Southerner between New Orleans and New York have followed suit.

By the end of 1940 Diesel passenger locomotives in the United States had approximately fifty million miles of service record behind them. The design of the locomotive had been standardized so that it was possible for manufacturers to begin to institute price reductions possible through the mass production principle of issuing numbers of copies of an accepted model. The result was that railroad executives could survey the mass of evidence accumulated in seven years and come to some definite conclusions as to the value of the Diesel on the rails. At this writing there remained some railroad operating men who still questioned the conclusions of their brothers who had been operating Diesels over long periods. The following observations, therefore, cannot be said to be universally accepted. However, it appears that the experience of the roads which have tried Diesels in various services over from three- to seven-year periods indicates the following:

Because of its higher availability (freedom from necessity for frequent major servicing and repair operations), one Diesel passenger locomotive will do the work, broadly speaking, of two steam locomotives.

Diesels, because of their more rapid accelerating ability in the lower speed brackets, long runs between fueling and other servicing operations, and ability to take curves at higher safe speeds due to their lower center of gravity, can economically operate trains on somewhat faster schedules than any but the most up-to-the-minute steam units.

Fuel and other operating costs, as well as maintenance costs, are about 50 per cent those of steam locomotives assigned to relatively comparable service. Exactly comparable figures are not available because nowhere in the world are steam locomotives assigned to such gruelling service as, for instance, the 39¾-hour, 2225-mile runs of the nine Diesel trains in operation in 1941 between Chicago and the Pacific Coast.

The original price of Diesel passenger locomotives is about twice that of a steam locomotive of comparable power, irrespective of whether the steam locomotive can do the same fast schedule work as the Diesel. Diesel backers contend that this higher first cost is offset by diminished fuel consumption, Diesel availability, low maintenance cost, and other economic assets.

It appears that passenger Diesels, in order to be most advantageously used, must be assigned to from six to eight hundred miles a day of regular service. Regardless of how many steam locomotives they replace, Diesel enthusiasts contend that the economies of Diesel operation, when in effect from six to eight hundred miles a day, pay out on the higher first price of the locomotive. This would seem to preclude the present type of mainline passenger locomotives from branch-line and shorter mainline runs, unless there is sufficient business to warrant two or more round trips a day. A number of experiments in the application of Diesel to these shorter, less obviously fertile operations, are under way. These involve Diesel locomotives of types other than the sleekly streamlined, brightly painted equipment with which the public has grown familiar on the crack mainline trains. By lengthening the wheel base of a 1000-horsepower Diesel switching locomotive to provide better tracking and adding heating boilers, the manufacturers have provided a branch-line locomotive capable of maintaining a sixty-mile-an-hour speed and hauling either passengers or freight, which is in operation upon some western railroads.

With none of the fanfare that has accompanied the infiltration of Diesel into mainline passenger service, it has made even more rapid strides in the switching field. The high availability, plus more rapid

AN ERA ENDS AND BEGINS HERE

The Atchison, Topeka and Santa Fe's 4500-horsepower, quadruple unit Diesel-electric locomotive No. 100 when it made its first revenue run between the Pacific Coast and Chicago early in 1941 broke a tradition of steam power for transcontinental freight hauls of more than seventy years' standing. The placing in revenue service of this type of power by the Santa Fe marked the invasion by Diesel-electric of every field of rail transport, as power in commuting service, on transcontinental and lesser fast varnish runs, in yard and switching operations, and head-end on redball freight. No. 100, shown here at the precise highest point in the Cajon in the San Bernardino Mountains on its initial trip east with 110 reefers and other high cars, is 193 feet long, weighs, when loaded with sand and fuel, 428 tons and is capable of sustained speeds of more than seventy-five miles an hour with a maximum load. The power plant of No. 100 comprises four sixteen-cylinder, two-cycle engines, each rated at 1350 horsepower. Direct current electric generators are connected with the crankshaft of each engine and the current from the four generators is fed to sixteen traction motors located in the trucks and geared directly to sixteen driving axles resulting in power application at thirty-two wheel-rail meeting points. Wide bands of yellow dominate the color scheme of the units which closely conform in outline and design to the profiles of Santa Fe passenger locomotives powered by Diesel.

Lucius Beebe photograph

THE 400 IN TRANSITION

er left:
H. Kindig
ograph

The Chicago and North Western Railway, famed for its English tradition of left-hand operations throughout its vast system, placed in operation on the Chicago–Twin Cities daily run on January 2, 1935, the fastest train at that time in regular passenger service in America, calling it the 400. It was then a five-car train powered by E-2 Pacific type locomotives reconditioned for high speed service with 79-inch cross-counter balanced drive wheels and new rod assemblies. The engines were oil-burners, and seven hours were consumed on the run operating at an average speed of 58.4 miles an hour including three five-minute stops. To-day

er left:
:ago and
th Western
ograph

the 400 consists of ten cars and the run is made behind 4000-horsepower two-unit Diesel-electric locomotives, built by the Electro-Motive Corporation, in six hours and fifteen minutes or an average speed of 65.4 miles an hour. The exterior color scheme of to-day's streamlined 400 is a brilliant yellow and green, and its luxury consist includes a de luxe diner, a tavern-lounge car, parlor cars, coaches, and a parlor-observation car. The photographs show the 400 in three successive stages of transition: with conventional steam power, with Diesel-electric motive-power before its streamlined cars were placed in service, and, finally, completely streamlined as it appears to-day.

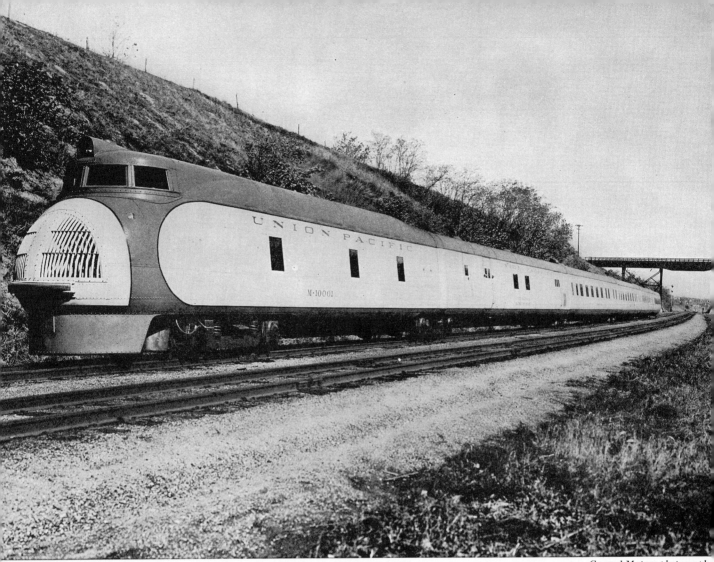

General Motors photograph

VETERAN OF THE DIESEL GENERATION

The City of Portland, second only in age to the venerable Pioneer Zephyr, gathers acceleration as it heads westward out of Omaha on the storied iron of the Union Pacific. In its first youth in 1934 while on a demonstration tour, the City of Portland set the transcontinental record of 56 hours and 55 minutes from coast to coast.

William Barham–Ivan Oaks photograph

STUDY IN STREAMLINING

Running on parallel tracks as they enter St. Louis, the Chicago, Burlington and Quincy's Mark Twain Zephyr on the St. Louis–Kansas City run and the Illinois Central's Green Diamond on the St. Louis–Chicago haul, present an interesting contrast in airflow design as they head west and north respectively the first thing each morning. The Green Diamond was an early pioneer in the Diesel-electric field and looks the part, but the Mark Twain Zephyr actually went into service six months before it, its more esthetically satisfactory lines and the continuance of its general style throughout the entire fleet of Burlington streamliners probably accounting for its newer appearance.

William Barham–Ivan Oaks photogra

OLD TIMER ON THE C. & E. I.

This Chicago and Eastern Illinois Atlantic No. 204 was photographed at the head end of Train 123, the Southern Illinois Express, southbound at Tamms, Illinois. This venerable 4-4-2 was built back in 1905 and is one of the three still in service on this road, and the picture has a pleasantly nostalgic atmosphere of the railroading of yesteryear.

THE SANTA FE IN COLORADO

Behind this Santa Fe Mountain type locomotive with a sleeve on its stack and its side rods gleaming are the six cars of the Centennial Limited as its hogger notched his throttle at a comfortable sixty between Denver and Castle Rock.

Upper right:
R. H. Kindi
photograph

EASTBOUND FROM ST. LOUIS

is this Louisville and Nashville six-car varnish entering a block near Belleville, Illinois, as the descending semaphore arm indicates. The engine is a light Pacific, No. 272, running with too little smoke for a photographer's satisfaction, although the picture is practically perfect from an operations department viewpoint.

Lower right:
William Bar
–Ivan Oaks
photograph

A VETERAN OF THE IRON

This Wabash Pacific, powering Train 23 near Anglum, Missouri, was converted in 1917 from a Prairie type (2-6-2) and was originally built in 1899. It was still able to make 75 miles an hour when this speed shot was taken while the fireboy waved a friendly greeting at the photographer.

REELING OFF THE COLORADO MILES

Perhaps the finest and most beautifully appointed of all the Rock Island's fleet of Diesel-electric Rockets is the Rocky Mountain Rocket with its Pullman-built sleepers, its lounges, diners, and observation cars, running in direct overnight competition with the Burlington's Budd-built Denver Zephyrs and the Union Pacific–Chicago and North Western City of Denver, all on the Chicago–Colorado run. The Rocky Mountain Rocket with a single power unit and seven black and silver cars setting out on the 1083-mile run to Chicago is climbing a slight grade in the rolling Colorado uplands at Derby.

LEAVING DENVER BEHIND

This interesting little varnish haul, powered by one of the Rock Island's red and silver Diesel-electric units, is the Rocky Mountain Special, a train which flourishes during the months when tourist travel is popular in the Colorado uplands.

A SILVER GREYHOUND STEPS OUT

The Sam Houston Zephyr–Texas Rocket, jointly operated by the Burlington and Rock Island, slips out of the Fort Worth yards on its daily 566 mile run on the Fort Worth–Dallas–Houston haul. In operation since 1935 the two units of this train are the original Twin Zephyrs operated in various services since they were released from the Chicago–Minneapolis run.

Lucius Beebe photograph

ORANGE, SILVER, PURPLE, AND GOLD TRIM

is the glittering color scheme of the Atlantic Coast Line's triple unit Diesel-electric locomotives pulling the standard coach and Pullman consist of the Florida Special between Washington and Miami. Shown here running with seventeen cars during the height of the Florida winter season near Hollywood, Florida, the Special is one of the oldest established overnight varnish trains between the north and Florida's east coast resorts, traversing in its passage the iron of the Pennsylvania R. F. & P., the Atlantic Coast Line itself, and the Flagler iron of the Florida East Coast.

GRAVEYARD RUN

The Peoria and Pekin Union Railway Company is an intermediate switching line serving fourteen railroads in central Illinois, and this not overesthetic Forney type 2-4-6 engine handling a lone coach and running tank first is on its final run into Peoria before being scrapped. It had formerly been on the power roster of the Illinois Central.

ROCKY MOUNTAIN BLUEBLOOD

Handsome and powerful thoroughbreds are the Denver and Rio Grande Western's race of 4-8-4s. Built for dual service in freight and passenger runs over divisions where the ruling grades are those of the Colorado Rockies, they are immaculately groomed and thoroughly shop-conditioned at all times. No. 1705 (note the head shack's shanty on the tender) is drifting up a slight grade coming into Littleton, Colorado, with No. 3, the Westerner, with cars for Memphis and Birmingham, Kansas City, St. Louis, and Chicago. The smoke deflector, solid sheet pilot, and silvered cylinder heads are characteristic details of Rio Grande power.

Upper right:
Lucius Beebe
photograph

ON THE COMMUTING RUN

On its suburban runs out of Boston, the Boston and Albany uses a number of these Forney 4-4-6 engines front end forward or tender first, impartially, to save the trouble of turning them. This one is clattering along headed for Huntington Avenue and the South Station near Newton Center, Massachusetts.

Lower right:
Lucius Beebe
photograph

NO PANTOGRAPH RISES HERE

Under the looping catenaries of the greatest electrified railroad system in the world, steam power still rises above change and refuses to acknowledge the mutations of time. A Pennsy Mountain type steam locomotive, Class M-Ia, designed for fast freight service, pounds down the main at Princeton Junction, New Jersey, ahead of 110 empty company hopper cars clanking back to the coal regions of Pennsylvania and West Virginia. The Pennsy still uses steam along its electrified main lines on through freights and local passenger hauls to save engine changes where trains turn onto unelectrified branch lines.

FAR CRY FROM LINK AND PIN

The tight lock coupling and rubber draft gear of one of the Pullmans of the Twentieth Century Limited show scant resemblance to the pre-Janney link and pin arrangements which once prevailed on every railroad in the United States. Besides the draw bar itself, inter-car connections on modern trains are provided by air brake and signal lines, emergency chain connections, telephone lines, and steam heating pipes.

Paul H. Stringham photograph

"FLEETER OF FOOT THAN THE FLEET-FOOT KID"

There are, as this is being written, fifteen Rockets serving the Middle West over the far-flung routes of the Rock Island Lines. They include the magnificent Rocky Mountain Rocket (pictured elsewhere in this volume), the Chocktaw Rocket, and the Zephyr Rocket, run in conjunction with the Burlington on the St. Louis–Twin Cities haul. Shown here is the Peoria Rocket powered by Diesel-electric No. 601, hitting better than sixty near Mossville, Illinois.

NO TRANSCENDENT BEAUTY

*pper left:
eneral Motors
otograph*

This is one of the sixteen early model two-car gasoline trains built between 1905 and 1915 for Union Pacific by the McKeen Motor Car Company and still in operation in 1941. Fresh from the back shops and newly brave in yellow and brown on the mainline west of Omaha, it is still no thing of radiant beauty although the lineal predecessor of such handsome internal-combustion units as those of the Rockets and Zephyrs, Super Chief and 400s.

HIGH IN THE RATON

*wer left:
H. Kindig
otograph*

Steam power enthusiasts might like to imagine this shot illustrates a breakdown of Diesel power. Unhappily for traditionalists, such is not the case. It is merely one of the Santa Fe's accustomed helpers, No. 920, a 2-10-2, a coal burner, on the head end of El Capitan passing through Wootton, Colorado, the highest point in the celebrated pass that is part of the storied Santa Fe Trail.

IN DEEPEST ESSEX COUNTY

The smoke deflectors on the Delaware and Hudson's passenger locomotives give them a distinctly continental air just as their poppet valve gear and high working boiler-pressure—in some cases 325 pounds—make them unique in the field of American motive-power. This is the second Laurentian, southbound at dusk passing through historic Essex County, New York. The train is the second section, a camper's special, of the road's day train between Montreal and Albany where its consist is taken over by the New York Central for the remainder of the run into New York. Despite appearances, the D. & H. customarily observes right hand operations, the track in the foreground being merely a passing track.

CINDERELLA OF THE RAILS

Before its transformation in the Chicago and Eastern Illinois shops this unusually handsome, streamlined Pacific, No. 1008, was regularly in service with conventional steam locomotive lines between Chicago and St. Louis. When the C. & E. I. undertook to run a through luxury coach train, the Dixie Flagler, from Chicago to Florida, it was rebuilt in the striking manner shown above. Elsewhere the Dixie Flagler is shown arriving in southern climes behind a Diesel-electric unit.

acceleration, and low operating costs of the Diesel, have made it practically a "natural" for switching, and by the middle of 1940 close to a
thousand were on American rails. One of the remarkable by-products
of Diesel switching has been their capitalization in advertising. Some
railroads, notably the Lehigh Valley, have decorated their Diesel switching locomotives used in passenger terminals with striking color schemes
to draw attention to progress on the road. Other railroads paint advertising messages on the flat smooth sides of their Diesel switchers. Since
they operate almost wholly in populous centers, they constitute one of
the best poster boards available to the railroads. Some railroads that
have become extensive users of Diesel switchers cite figures to show that
operating and maintenance savings over steam operation save the price
of the Diesel in from two and a half to four years. Confirmed steam-
power believers concede Diesel supremacy in the field of yard operations.

But could the Diesel engine be applied to the principal job of the railroads, freight service? Three times as many locomotives are used in
American freight service as in passenger service. Here was the biggest
job to be done, and if the Diesel economies could be applied to it, for-
ward-looking railroad executives saw the possibility of a powerful weapon
in the battle to rehabilitate railroad financial structures, as well as a tool
with which to make possible, ultimately, better public service.

Early in 1939, Hamilton's organization at Electro-Motive completed
its first experimental model of a 5400-horsepower freight locomotive.
They loaned it in turn to some twenty Class 1 railroads from coast to
coast for trials on each road on runs regarded either as the toughest or
the most typical jobs their freight motive-power had to do. The locomotive was designed along the same lines as mainline passenger locomotives, particularly as to construction in sections. The 5400-horsepower
locomotive can be broken up into two 2700-horsepower locomotives or
one 1300-horsepower and one 4050-horsepower, providing flexibility that
fits the horsepower to the job to be done.

The experimental model piled up an impressive record in eleven
months. And once more the Santa Fe, pioneer in other spectacular
applications of Diesel, added another "first" to its record. It ordered
two of these Giant Jeeps as they were playfully dubbed upon their first

public appearance. The Santa Fe put the first of these locomotives in general freight duty on various divisions between Chicago and Los Angeles in February, 1940. Thus the Santa Fe became the first railroad in the world to apply Diesel motive-power to all classes of service—switching, passenger, and freight.

The new locomotive set up a spectacular record on its first revenue run from Kansas City to Los Angeles, with seventy cars totalling 3000 tons. The locomotive cut over fifty hours off the regular schedule for the fastest transcontinental freight train. It showed up, as it had in the eleven months of its trial period, particularly well in hauling heavy tonnage up long mountain grades. Its ability quickly to accelerate heavy tonnage and keep it moving at the locomotive's top speed of seventy-five miles an hour on the prairie divisions also counted heavily in time-saving. Shortly thereafter the Southern Railroad, the Great Northern, the Western Pacific, the Chicago Milwaukee, St. Paul and Pacific, and the Seaboard placed initial orders. The Santa Fe on the basis of its experience with its first two units placed an additional order for this type of equipment which at that time stood as the largest single order for Diesel equipment in the history of the business.

The possibilities of better public service with the new freight locomotives are difficult to forecast because so many other factors enter into the speeding up of freight service than simply the motive-power. However, experienced railroad men on western railroads professed to see fifth morning delivery out of Chicago in Los Angeles and San Francisco, in place of sixth morning then in force, as a relatively easy possibility. The day when through freight might ultimately be moving as second sections of fast passenger trains did not seem so remote as theretofore.

The daily high-speed schedules totaling over twenty million miles a year of the 140 Diesel-powered passenger trains operating in the United States by late in 1941 were spectacular enough to serve as a hall mark of the remarkable progress of American railroads during the depression decade. Some of the individual achievements of some of these trains serve as highlights of the record, however.

The Pioneer Zephyr of the Burlington on May 26, 1934, ran non-stop the 1015 miles from Denver to the Century of Progress Exposition at

Chicago in 13 hours and 5 minutes, an average speed of 77.5 miles per hour. One of the Burlington's longer, heavier, and more powerful Denver Zephyr sleeper trains shattered this record on October 23, 1936, when it negotiated the same 1015-mile run in 12 hours and 12 minutes, at an average speed of 83.3 miles per hour, reaching a top speed of 116 miles per hour and covering one 27-mile stretch at 105.8 miles per hour. This stood at the time this book was published as the world's long-distance record for both average speed and non-stop.

Other spectacular long-distance records set by Diesel trains were: City of Portland of the Chicago and North Western and Union Pacific, on October 22, 1934, 3258 miles from Los Angeles to New York in 56 hours 55 minutes, an average of 57.2 miles per hour; Super Chief of the Santa Fe, on May 17, 1937, from Los Angeles to Chicago, 2228 miles in 36 hours and 49 minutes, average speed of 60.5 miles per hour including seventeen stops, with one stretch from La Junta, Colorado, to Dodge City, Kansas (known to Santa Fe operating men as "The Speedway"), of 202 miles at an average of 87.2 miles per hour.

One of the Burlington's Chicago–St. Paul–Minneapolis Twin Zephyrs made the 431 miles from Chicago to St. Paul in 5 hours and 33 minutes, an average of 77.6 miles per hour on April 6, 1935.

While time and further experience may dictate changes, it appears that certain definite horsepower ranges for Diesel units for regular railroad service have become established. Diesel switchers are made, generally, in 300-, 600-, and 1000-horsepower units; branch-line locomotives in 1000-horsepower sizes; transfer locomotives, 2000-horsepower, main-line passenger, 2000-horsepower, and freight in 1350- and 2700-horsepower units. In the case of passenger and freight locomotives the units, which term could be more popularly understood if the word cars were used, can be quickly coupled together to give any desired multiple. Thus there are 2000 (one unit), 4000 (two unit) and 6000 (three unit) Diesel passenger locomotives in service and freight locomotives of 2700-, 4050-, and 5400-horsepower.

The fact that there are many Diesel passenger locomotives of 6000-horsepower, whereas the most powerful freight locomotive is 5400 horsepower, is confusing to many persons who cannot see why the higher horsepower is not assigned to the freight locomotive which has to start and haul far heavier weights. Peculiarly enough, the 5400-horsepower Diesel freight locomotives will easily start and pull to fast cruising speed many times the weight which the 6000-horsepower passenger locomotive can move. The difference in ability lies in the difference in design of the electric transmission. The electric transmission in the passenger locomotive is designed to accelerate to top speed in the quickest possible time the relatively light weight of the heaviest passenger train, normally not more than eighteen standard Pullman sleepers. These locomotives have a top rated speed with full load of about 117 miles an hour. They have gone somewhat faster. The freight locomotives, on the other hand, are not expected to pull their heavy loads faster than 75 miles an hour. So the electric transmission on the freight locomotive is designed to concentrate the application of power on the job of starting the heavy loads and lugging them up grades at good speed, sacrificing speed in the higher ranges. Perhaps the difference can be better understood by comparison with the transmissions of ordinary passenger automobiles and trucks. A passenger automobile with a 100-horsepower engine has a transmission that permits it to go as high as 100 miles an hour. The self-same engine in a motor truck designed to haul three or four tons of goods probably will not get up much over 60 miles an hour with full load, the difference lying in the gearing.

In the case of the Diesel freight locomotives, the designers found that 5400-horsepower was approximately the most economical high point for power. There would be no point in installing 6000-horsepower and burning the fuel necessary to keep engines of this size running if 5400-horsepower would do the job.

In the midst of all this discussion of Diesel-electric motive-power and its many apparent advantages in the filling of specialized transportation functions, it has not been the writer's intention to devote space to this new type of power at the expense of adequate appreciation of the current and certain-to-be-continued uses of steam. The circumstance simply is that he devoted an equally lengthy chapter to conventional power in an earlier volume (*High Iron, A Book of Trains*, 1938).

At the current writing the Electro-Motive Corporation boasts that it is the dominant manufacturer of railroad locomotives of the world, and, while this may well be so, it has been unable to sell to either the Union Pacific or Southern Pacific any such impressive bill of goods as it has to the Santa Fe. Only recently the American Locomotive Company at Schenectady reported the placing by the U. P. for immediate delivery an order for twenty steam locomotives which for size, speed, and horsepower dwarf anything yet constructed in the field of freight transportation. Details of these locomotives have not been released but it is understood they are to have a rating of 7000 horsepower, a boiler pressure of 300 pounds, be capable of achieving a cruising speed of eighty miles an hour and a comparable tractive force over the ruling grades of the Wasatch Mountains in Utah and Wyoming with maximum pay loads. Considered in the light of other vast orders for freight power in steam by any number of Class 1 roads such as the Southern Pacific and Western Maryland, the record of Diesel-electric freight power construction is still in its veriest infancy.

Old-timers among railroad operating crews at the outset quite naturally had some difficulty in accustoming themselves to their surroundings in the cab of a Diesel locomotive. The century-old affection for the conventional Iron Horse is not by any means uprooted. The very intent of the designers of Diesel locomotives to make the jobs of engineers and firemen safer and easier is, at first, offensive to dyed-in-the-wool hoggers. A certain masculine quality about the job of wrestling a powerful steam locomotive over a division through foul weather or fair seems to be lacking in the sleekly comfortable job in the cab of a Diesel. Yet the old-timers seem to like their Diesel jobs once they have held them for a short time.

The engineer and firemen of Diesel road locomotives sit in padded, leather-upholstered, swivel arm-chairs, scientifically designed for the greatest bodily comfort over an eight-hour tour of duty. Their stations are high in the nose of the locomotive, placed several feet back of the front anti-climb bumper. This position was fixed by regard not only for the finest possible vision of right-of-way but also with an eye to the safety of the operating crew in case of collision. The actual nose of the locomotive protruding below and for several feet in front of the position of the operators is armored and braced as if it were going to be used for a battering ram.

The essential controls of a Diesel locomotive are the same as those on a steam locomotive, the result of deliberate plan on the part of the builders to make it possible for steam engineers to swing over to Diesel operation after two or three instruction trips. These essential controls are the throttle, reverse lever, train brake, and locomotive brake levers. One additional control lever is provided on the Diesel freight locomotive. This lever changes phases in the traction motors, but with the aid of an illuminated indicator engineers who know nothing whatever about the intricacies of electricity learn its proper operation in a day or so. Engineers assigned to Diesel are not sent to schools to learn Diesel operation. They climb into the cab and are familiarized with the job on regular runs by instructors who either spell them at the throttle or stand behind them giving advice.

One additional safety device is provided on Diesel road locomotives not ordinarily found on steam locomotives. This is the emergency control pedal, or as popularly known, dead-man control. This control consists of a depressable throttle lever and a foot pedal. The engineer must keep either the foot pedal or the throttle lever depressed or power is automatically shut off and an emergency brake application is made. The purpose of this, obviously, is protection of the train in case the engineer becomes incapacitated. The control is provided through either the throttle or the foot pedal in order to lessen the chance of operator fatigue. The engineer can rest his foot by releasing the pressure on the foot pedal and pressing on the throttle handle.

Cabs are heated by steam or electricity in cold weather and cooled by no-draft ventilator windows on each side in hot weather. Automatic windshield wipers with a de-icing fluid and the same type of channel windshield defrosters used in modern automobiles are installed. Long sun visors are in place for protection when riding into the early morning or late afternoon sun. The partition and door between the cab and the engine room immediately behind it are insulated and the roof of the cab acoustically treated to keep out and deaden track and engine noises. It is possible for engineer and fireman, seated about six feet across the cab from each other, to exchange signal observations and converse in tones just slightly stronger than those used in ordinary conversation. The crew members may smoke in the cab if they choose, there being no fire hazard.

An instrument board, similar to that on an airplane, is placed immediately in front of the engineer. Indicators for speed, air pressure, wheel slip, abnormal condition in the Diesel equipment, and hot journals are provided. Some locomotives on de luxe transcontinental trains are equipped with telephones for conversation with the conductor or other crew members back in the passenger cars.

Simply stated, the Diesel locomotive consists of a Diesel engine as the primary source of power, an electrical generator connected directly to and driven by it, traction motors operated by current from the generator, the necessary controlling apparatus, a car to house them in, and trucks to carry the whole. The traction motors are located in the trucks and are geared directly to the driving axles.

The major equipment in a typical Electro-Motive 2000-horsepower passenger unit consists of: two 1000-horsepower, two-cycle General Motors Diesel engines, two direct-current generators, four traction motors, two six-wheel trucks, engine-cooling equipment such as radiators and fans (located in the car roof), tanks for engine fuel and for train-heating boiler, and the necessary controlling apparatus.

Ingenious apparatus is built in for the control of the power. The engineer does not regulate the speed of the train by revving up the Diesel engine as is popularly supposed. He has no direct control over what the Diesel engine is doing in the room back of him. He merely manipulates his throttle and the controls necessary to make the locomotive respond with either more power to pull up a grade or to go faster operate automatically. In unscientific terms, what happens, roughly, is this: the engineer "telegraphs" to the traction motors in the trucks that he wants them to speed up, pull harder, or slow down when he moves the throttle. The automatic equipment makes the Diesel engine run fast or slow enough to turn the generator so as to make the right amount of current to permit the traction motors to do what the engineer has "ordered" them to do.

Electro-Motive Diesels are not only equipped with shock absorbers to abate perpendicular motion but also with lateral springing, located in the journals, to absorb sidesway. This not only makes for a smooth forward motion on straight track but also helps to eliminate jerks and sidesway on curves because the side springs absorb the side shock when the locomotive enters or leaves a curve. This type of springing, plus the low center of gravity, are factors in the Diesel locomotive's ability to take curves with safety and passenger comfort at higher speeds.

Servicing practice varies, but generally speaking, Diesel passenger locomotives run from five to six hundred miles without refueling, some farther. The Diesel freight locomotive is designed to haul five thousand tons five hundred miles without a fuel stop. Stops for water for the train heating boiler depend upon the weather. Normally there is a total of six service stops of about five minutes each for the locomotives on the 2225-mile Chicago to Pacific Coast runs. Locomotives are not changed on these or any other Diesel runs, regardless of length. It is not necessary to withdraw the Diesel from service frequently for major servicing operations such as firebox cleaning, boiler washing, and the like such as are standard practice on steam equipment. Two 4000-horsepower Diesels on the Chicago and North Western ran in night and day service on two different high-speed trains—one a semi-light-weight de luxe day train and the other a heavy Pullman sleeper train—totalling approximately 875 miles a day for fourteen months before either missed a trip for repairs. Several Diesel locomotives have been operated close to a million miles before being withdrawn for major overhaul. Most Diesel road units are operated about a half-million miles before major overhaul is necessary. By way of comparison, it may be noted that it is general practice to bring steam locomotives in for major overhaul at from 100,000 to 125,000 miles.

This does not mean, of course, that some repairs are not necessary upon Diesel road locomotives. But most of the repairs that have to be made before major overhaul are of such a minor nature and the design of the locomotive make the parts so accessible that the work is easily done during the few hours between scheduled runs. In some instances on long fast schedules this turn-around period is as low as six hours. Some of the locomotives on transcontinental runs will reach Chicago or Los Angeles at around 8:00 or 9:00 A.M. and start out on another 2225 mile jaunt at 6:00 or 7:00 the same evening week after week, month after month, without missing a trip. Some railroads include a mechanic, called a maintainer in the engine-rooms of Diesels on long runs. These men can make minor repairs as the train speeds on. Several instances are on record in which service men actually changed a cylinder liner, piston, or connecting-rod on one of the big Diesels with the train roaring ahead on the power of the remaining Diesels. Any of the engines in a multiple-unit locomotive can be cut out by simply pushing a stop button. The design of the engine used in the Electro-Motive type of Diesel locomotive is such that pistons, liners, and connecting-rods can be changed easily inside the engine-room and with the train in motion.

If it is deemed inadvisable or impossible to make a repair on an engine during a run the crew merely leaves that engine cut out and goes on to the terminal on the remaining power, and repairs are made on arrival.

Persons unfamiliar with standard railroad practices sometimes have the idea that there is something lacking in Diesel locomotives because now and then they discover that steam boosters regularly help famous Diesel trains over long mountain passes. The uninitiated goes home and tells his friends that the Diesel locomotive hasn't got enough power to get over the grades. The truth is that all trains are helped over such grades. It is equally true that steam locomotives, or Diesel locomotives, powerful enough to pull passenger trains at the desired speeds up long steep grades readily could be provided. In the case of a Diesel all that is necessary is to just couple another unit into the locomotive. This expedient would, however, be uneconomic. A good case example to demonstrate just how unsuitable is the Santa Fe Diesel operation between Chicago and Los Angeles. Steam boosters help the crack Santa Fe Diesel trains over three famous passes in the San Bernardino and Rocky Mountains— the Raton, Glorieta, and Cajon. These grades total about seventy-five miles. The regular 3600- and 4000-horsepower Diesels are adequate to maintain the high-speed service over all the rest of the 2225-mile run. It would be highly uneconomic to carry the extra horsepower needed on the seventy-five miles of extra steep mountain grades over those 2150 miles in which there is no earthly use for it. So the railroad stations one or two booster locomotives at the spots where the extra power is needed for practically every train, freight or passenger, that comes along, instead of spending the enormous sum that would be necessary to add the extra horsepower to every locomotive, steam or Diesel, that may ever have occasion to run over these tough grades.

The Diesel with its greater flexibility, economy, speed, and availability has won its place on American railroads. Research continues in two major directions which may make the Diesel locomotive an even more useful tool. One major project aims at high-powered Diesel engines in smaller sizes than now available, the other at elimination of the costly electric transmission. Success in either of these developments would materially reduce the cost of such locomotives because either the size or number of cars needed to carry the propulsion machinery would be cut in addition to the machinery itself.

Lucius Beebe photograph

Lucius Beebe photograph

3
Varnish Vignettes

THE CANNONBALL stoves on the Bangor and Aroostook coaches of the writer's boyhood, souvenirs of a wooden coach era when the least derailment implied a possible holocaust. . . . The wonderful fresh mountain trout, direct from the icy streams of the Colorado Rockies, served on the diners of the Denver and Rio Grande Western's Scenic Limited as it passed over the roof of the western world. . . . The dining-car steward aboard the old Florida Special en route to Palm Beach reminding the writer's father that it was his fortieth wedding anniversary. . . . He'd been a waiter captain in the Vendome Hotel in Boston four decades previous. . . . Riding 100 miles an hour headend on the Santa Fe's Chief on the speedway out of La Junta and being black and blue for a fortnight as a result. . . . The restaurant cars on the new Twentieth Century Limited which, by switching the table linen and lights to a subdued orchid, become night clubs after ten o'clock in the evening. . . . Miscalculating the speed of the Morning Hiawatha while taking speed shots at Lake Forest, Illinois, and losing a good new hat in the draft created by its passing. . . . The service of five o'clock tea, *à l'anglais,* aboard the Pullmans and first-class coaches of the Lackawanna. . . . The thrice welcome hods of beer on Edward Hungerford's air-cooled Pullman which served as press headquarters at the New York World's Fair showing of "Railroads on Parade." . . . The whistle of the nightly New Britain freight, a wistful souvenir of undergraduate days at New Haven. . . . The chicken stew, magnificent with dumplings, served by a singing darky waiter on the Wabash Banner Blue while passing through the Illinois cornfields one summer afternoon. . . . The inscribed white overalls, cap, and driver's gloves presented to the writer by the St. Louis Terminal Association Employees at the dedication of the new interlocking there. . . . The writer's delight at being able to train a camera on the Alton–Burlington's General Pershing Zephyr being shamefully hauled out of Kansas City on the St. Louis run by a veteran Burlington Pacific. . . . Drinking vintage wine with the tailcoated governors of

145

four states aboard a Colorado and Southern private car at Blackhawk, Colorado, during the Central City Festival. . . . The writer breaking his nose when he was thrown from his berth on the Chesapeake and Ohio's Sportsman when the driver pulled a drawbar in the middle of the night near Manassas. . . . The splendid paint jobs on the Frisco's power with its burnished brass, blue sheen of boiler lagging, and red and gold number markers. . . . The electric clocks, private room radios, and other travel luxuries on the Burlington's Denver Zephyr, most beautiful of the early streamliners. . . . Standing with President Williamson of the Central on the brass-railed observation platform of the old Century as it overtook a hotshot slamming out of Elkhart, Indiana, and the old gentleman saying: "Look at those high cars roll; finest sight in the world!" . . . The courtesy of an old-time conductor on the Southern's Queen and Crescent who held his train five minutes somewhere in the wilds of Mississippi so the writer could finish in comfort a mess of shrimps Creole. . . . The open platform coaches and forty-year old 4-4-0s and 2-6-0s on the Western Division of the Boston and Maine which came straight from some lithographic railroading scene of the seventies or eighties. . . . Waiting for the Chief, working steam and with Johnson bars notched all the way forward on road engine and helper, in the Cajon and knowing that the action shot of a lifetime was coming up the grade, cold turkey. . . . The old days when as many as twenty private cars at a time were spotted on the house tracks of the now vanished Royal Poinciana Hotel at Palm Beach. . . . Even the trestle across Lake Worth has gone now. . . . The elaborate club cars on the Mopac's Sunshine Special, decorated in Mission style with a bar, soda fountain, reading compartment, observation lounge, shower bath, and everything but a swimming plunge. . . . Encountering once aboard the U.P.'s City of Denver a steward who had been the writer's Uncle Marc's butler long since. . . . Passing through Tobar on the Western Pacific at the southern end of the Great Salt Lake, now just a sign to commemorate a town named in the seventies for its principal direction post whose legend read "To Bar." . . . The handsomest of all club cars on the Pennsy's Broadway Limited, designed and decorated by Raymond Loewy with historic murals instead of windows and a color theme of the Pennsy's celebrated Tuscan red. . . . Riding in mortal terror in the

COLLECTOR'S ITEM

Although the Gulf, Mobile and Ohio's streamlined Rebel and Gulf Stream Rebel are well known to railroad photographers, freight shots along this Middle West–gulf port railroad are, for some inscrutable reason, comparatively rare. Here is the G. M. & O.'s veteran No. 405, a Mikado with a tank car for extra water behind the tender, as it wheels southward through the early morning mists of the river bottoms near Milstadt Junction, Illinois. Both members of the head-end crew have crowded to the fireman's window to see what goes on.

Paul H. Stringham photograph

OLD TIMER OF THE RAILS

is this Rogers-built 4-6-0, Class K-2 muzzle-loader of the Chicago, Burlington and Quincy with its high domes, square steam chests, stovepipe smokestack and ancient headlight mounted above the smokebox. It was photographed at Edwards, Illinois, west of Peoria at thirty-five miles an hour at the smoky end of mixed train No. 11 with four cars on the Peoria to Buda run.

VETERAN HIGH STEPPER OF THE C. & E. I.

These immaculate and thoroughbred light Pacifics of the Chicago and Eastern Illinois are approximately thirty years old, but they are still among the most gallant and fastidiously shopped engines in Illinois. The St. Louis Zipper, on the daily Chicago–St. Louis run, has a tight schedule, covering the 290 miles between Dearborn Station and the St. Louis Terminal in a flat five hours. She is shown nearing the interlocking at the East St. Louis end of Merchant's Bridge doing seventy with a make-up of five standard-weight steel cars.

Upper right:
William Barhar
Ivan Oaks
photograph

ANCIENT OF RAILROADING DAYS

Unchanged in wheel arrangement and fundamental design since before the Civil War, the classic American type locomotive (4-4-0) still survives on branch lines of many of the railroads of the land, especially in the east and middle west. This veteran of the Chicago and Illinois Midland, No. 501, Class A-1, is wheeling a Peoria to Springfield local at about a mile a minute near Pekin, Illinois. Amateurs of the historic aspects of the high iron in many cases prefer to lavish their affections on such aged mills rather than on the sleekest and most up-to-the-minute Mountain types or Hudsons.

Lower right:
Paul H. String
photograph

IN A CLASS BY ITSELF

The ornamental lines and engineering grace notes of this Texas and Pacific class P-1r, built by Baldwin in 1919, distinguish it as the only locomotive of its kind in service throughout the system. Its boiler pressure is 200 pounds, its drivers 74 inches and it possesses a tractive effort of 40,200 pounds. Engines No. 701-713, constructed at the same time, are class P-1 and P-1a and are somewhat more powerful and heavy. No. 700 is taking the Sunshine Special, West Texas–California section, out of Fort Worth with the throttle well back and the power reverse gear in the "company notch." There are two other sections of the Sunshine, the South Texas–Mexico haul and the daily North Texas varnish which connects at Texarkana with the Missouri Pacific to run into St. Louis.

OVER THE TOP OF THE WORLD

From the Denver and Rio Grande Western's station in Santa Fe to Antonito,
Colorado, is 126 miles over the gloomy, winter-bound mountains of New Mexico
by way of Espanola and Taos Junction. On one of the few remaining narrow-
gage runs of the storied West, this outside frame Mikado, No. 473, is heading
for the snow-covered uplands out of Santa Fe with a four-car mixed consist and
a full head of steam, while a backdrop of storm clouds promise more snow before
the run is finished late in the afternoon.

B. & M. WESTERN DIVISION

Crossing the Wakefield-Reading, Massachusetts, town boundary line the Boston and Maine light Pacific, No. 3628, is rolling a holiday special from Boston to Portland with two Pullmans on the head end and a string of old-fashioned wooden coaches full of excursionists behind.

RIGHT OUT OF YESTERDAY

This narrow-gage vignette might have been taken in the eighties rather than in 1940, complete as it is with a Rio Grande, outside-frame Mikado, mixed consist, classic background of water tower and maintenance shack, and riverside roadbed. It was taken by Mr. Kindig as this interesting train was pulling out of Embudo, New Mexico, on the Santa Fe Branch of the D. & R. G. W.

ILLINOIS CENTRAL'S CRACK VARNISH

This handsome speed shot shows the I. C.'s Train No. 5, the Panama Limited, with Pacific 1135 on the smoky end and a company official's private car immediately behind the tender southbound over a viaduct near Watson, Illinois. A notable below-the-tracks angle shot.

THE WHISTLER OF THE BOXCARS

Boxcar art is largely indigenous to hobos, drifters, and migratory workers who establish a brief esthetic immortality with chalk writing and ideographs. Best known and most often imitated, however, is the hallmark and *fecit* of Bozo Texino, who in real life is J. H. McKinley, a Missouri Pacific engineman from San Antonio, Texas. For years he has been drawing, with an altogether characteristic flourish on the side of boxcars, a cowboy profile with a wide hat, sometimes with and sometimes without a long churchwarden pipe. Authorities on such matters can distinguish an authenic Bozo Texino from a spurious one as easily as a connoisseur can recognize a veritable Whistler butterfly. This specimen, probably no fabrication, but the work of the master himself, was detected on an International Great Northern high car rolling through the yards of the Santa Fe at San Bernardino, California.

BEFORE THE STREAMLINERS CAME

Sometime during the spacious and Victorian eighties in a pre-Raymond Loewy era this eight-wheeler puttered over the rails of the New York Central and Hudson River's Putnam Division with two coaches full of local passengers. Its heroic headlight, oval engineer's window, square steam chest and flanged domes proclaim its honorable vintage. The picture is probably a re-photograph of an original positive made from a wet plate developed on the scene by the photographer and is one of the few action railroad photographs in existence stemming from that decade.

ILLINOIS PASTORAL

En route to Louisville, 273 miles eastward, this little Southern Railroad train, No. 23, is shown heading into the early morning sun at Belleville, Illinois, a few miles east of St. Louis, behind light Pacific No. 1206.

Lucius Beebe photograph

SANTA FE SMOKE

Giving the photographer the satisfaction of a rolling smoke exhaust, this Atchison, Topeka and Santa Fe hogger is wheeling Train 101, the Centennial State, through Littleton, Colorado, en route to Colorado Springs, Pueblo, La Junta, Kansas City, and Chicago. A light train of five coaches and Pullmans is headed by a Mountain engine, No. 3719, of typical Santa Fe design. South out of Denver the mainline as far as Colorado Springs is used jointly by the Santa Fe, Colorado and Southern and Rio Grande.

NEVER AGAIN TO GEORGETOWN, TO SILVER PLUME

Not ever again will the patrons of French Louis duPuy's fabulous Hotel de Paris at Georgetown hear the startling bell on Colorado and Southern's Narrow-Gage No. 60, clap top hats on their heads and hasten to the depot for the mixed train to Denver town. Nor will the miners at Forkscreek mosey over to the post-office next the Placer Saloon after it has brought up the mail. The rails behind No. 60 and ahead of her have disappeared forever and it stands, a monument to the heroic past of the Rocky Mountain Empire on a fifty-foot section of sixty pound iron next the crumbling station at Idaho Springs, a ghostly locomotive, half way between nowhere and nowhere. A mile higher toward the Great Divide, at Central City, No. 71 is similarly immobile and similarly immortal. It may be that narrow-gage railroading, like French Louis and Haw Tabor and Baby Doe and all the wonderful characters of the Colorado saga have gone into the noth-ingness of the legendary past, but they will live on in the American chronicle and the American imagination, forever.

William Barham–Ivan Oaks photograph

CRACK COTTON BELT VARNISH

The exquisite little train wheeling its way north behind an immaculate Atlantic engine, No. 601, is the St. Louis Southwestern's (Cotton Belt) No. 6 between the cities of East Texas and St. Louis caught by the camera one sunrise near Dupo, Illinois. The high-stepping 4-4-2 was built in the early part of the century, but still is capable of whipping up a good seventy with the five cars of the Morning Star. Before being rechristened the train was known as the Cotton Belter.

GG-I, CLASSIC PENNSY ELECTRIC POWER

What the K4-s is to the roster of the Pennsylvania Railroad's steam motive-power, the GG-I, 4-6-0–0-6-4 engine is to the listing of the road's electric loco-motives. It is the most powerful electric passenger locomotive ever built and is monarch of the Pennsy's electrified divisions between New York, Philadelphia, Harrisburg, and Washington. Baldwin, General Electric, Westinghouse, and the railroad's own engineers coöperated in the design of GG-I, whose driving axles are powered by twin motors through double-end quill drive. Power is rated at 385 horse-power per armature, thus providing 770 per driving axle or 4620 horsepower at ninety miles an hour for the six power axles. The GG-I is designed for through passenger and fast freight service at speeds in excess of one hundred miles an hour and can develop 8000 horsepower for short periods of time. In the accom-panying photograph, taken at Metuchen, New Jersey, a GG-I is hustling toward New York with fifteen overnight Pullmans from Washington and connecting roads from the deep South.

Lucius Beebe photograph

BLUE BIRD IN FLIGHT

The Wabash's Blue Bird is the late afternoon passenger run between St. Louis and Chicago, Trains 24 and 21. The northbound section is here shown nearing Decatur, Illinois, where it will change engines for the run into Chicago. The Wabash is famed for its speed and commissary if not for modernity of passenger equipment, and for many years was known as a training school of celebrated railroad men.

cab of the General Bowker at Iron Springs, Utah, during the filming of Paramount's "Union Pacific" when the hogger on the big U.P. freight job that was hauling the train—complete with wooden coaches of Civil War vintage—forgot that the Bowker wasn't really good for fifty miles an hour and the wind tore the wooden cab off around our ears. There was no train line to signal him with, and we rode ten miles down the Lund spur clutching at the backhead gear and remembering past sins. . . . The remarkable railroad knowledge of Cecil B. DeMille, director of the film, who could detect technical flaws in the sets invisible even to President William Jeffers who watched part of the filming. . . . The view of Donner Lake under a frozen February moon seen from a drawing-room on the City of San Francisco through the passing snowsheds. . . . The sightly airflow lines of the green and gold 4-8-2s that power the Grand Trunk's Maple Leaf out of Chicago. . . . The Orange Blossom in three sections of eighteen cars each romping through the palmetto groves of Florida during the height of the southern season. . . . The tinted windows of the club and restaurant cars of the Texas and Pacific on the run between El Paso and East Texas to abate the glare of the desert sun. . . . The dining-car of the Forty-Niner, a full-length, ninety-foot restaurant with the kitchen in the next unit, reported once to have been the private conveyance of the President of Mexico. . . . The all-night party aboard W. Averell Harriman's twenty-car private train over the Illinois Central between Chicago and Omaha for a film junket. . . . The thrill implicit in the name Rio Grande whenever encountered on equipment in obscure yards at the ends of the continent. . . . The most sightly of all Diesel-electric units, the colorful and speedy seven-car Rocky Mountain Rocket on the Rock Island. . . . The state dinner arranged by the company aboard the City of Los Angeles for Lady Suzanne Wilkins, complete from caviar to soufflé and including trout, grouse, Mexican quail and vintage wines. . . . The first breath-catching sight of the Espee's Daylight, all orange and red and black, streaking over the ochre hillsides of California under a trailing cloud of black oil smoke as the hogger worked steam for the next grade. . . . The very de luxe restaurant-car service aboard the Illinois Central's Panama Limited with its fine crockery, menus printed on gold leaf paper, its specially uniformed waiters and profusion of cut flowers. . . . The broad lawn and colorful flowering shrubs between the two terminal tracks of the Colorado and Southern–Louisiana and Arkansas station at New Orleans. . . . The rebuilt K-4s power on the Pennsy's Jeffersonian, the first time a Pennsylvania steam unit has incorporated nickel steel cylinder heads, red and gold trim and a generally imaginative locomotive design. . . .

Lucius Beebe photograph

4
Super De Luxe

IT IS an engaging paradox that the rise of luxury rail transportation, the evolution of most of the actual trains themselves and almost all the equipment which come under the head of de luxe passenger travel, should be achieved in the midst of a nation-wide economic depression of unprecedented scope and duration. Of the more than half a hundred name trains now generally and popularly associated with more than average speed, styling, and resources of comfort and pleasure, only a handful would be recognized by the overland traveler of thirty years ago and scarcely a single one of them has the equipment identical with that used on the same run as recently as fifteen years ago. Changes in motive-power have been dramatic, but the consists of celebrated passenger runs have undergone mutations equally arresting and discernible to all the senses.

Thirty-five years ago, when the Pennsylvania's Broadway and the New York Central's Twentieth Century Limited were in their first flush of triumphant and—to the popular imagining—astounding youth, the New York, New Haven and Hartford's fabulous White Train on the New York–Boston run was already only a fragrant legend. Of the other eye-popping flyers of the era, the New Haven's Knickerbocker has been succeeded by the Yankee Clipper; the Atchison, Topeka and Santa Fe's California Limited is still carded, but has long since yielded place to the Chief and Super Chief; while the Union Pacific's Overland Limited has assumed an aspect of somewhat wayward mediocrity and homely comfort beside the glories of the City of Los Angeles and City of San Francisco. The Empire State Express of the Central and the Florida Special of the Florida East Coast line, the Broadway, the Century still flourish under their celebrated names but in transformed redactions which would scarcely be recognizable to their passengers at the turn of the century.

It took hard times, intense competition from other forms of passenger transportation, and the often drastic impertinences of agencies of the Federal Government to bring into being first-class trains out-shining the private car consists of industrial magnates of the earlier decades of the era and to create coach and tourist facilities which would have astonished luxury fare passengers of twenty years ago.

More than anything else in the matter of interior decorations of trains, there has never been any attempt to escape from the railroad motif with the possible exceptions of such frontier innovations as the Little Nugget Bar on the City of Los Angeles and the Frontier Shack on the City of Denver. Raymond Loewy, Henry Dreyfuss, and the other crack industrial designers, decorators, artists, and photomuralists employed in providing the esthetic overtones of modern rail travel, have never subscribed to the practice, so universal among ship builders of a generation ago and even more recently, of making their interiors resemble anything in the world but the locale in which they were actually situated. Ocean liners' lounges and saloons were fabricated in imitation of Ritz Carlton restaurants, Persian gardens, Scotch hunting lodges, Roman pavilions, Georgian libraries, Swiss chalets, Chinese pagodas, the Taj Mahal, Westminster Abbey, and Sloppy Joe's gin mill. Decorative motifs ranged from Rembrandt to Lalique and from Sir Joshua Reynolds to Toulouse-Lautrec; anything to obscure and diminish the circumstance that travelers were afloat in a sea-going ship. Stateroom suites resembled those of Claridge's in London, grand staircases recreated the spirit of the Paris Opera, portholes were replaced with French windows, and any suggestion of maritime existence was as assiduously abated as a wine salesman at a church supper.

Not so, however, with the realistic artists who have created the theme of the Broadway and Century, the Southern Belle, the Rockets, and the Super Chief. In them, railroads and railroading are the dominant motif, usually interwoven with historical and contemporary aspects of the regions and cities through which they pass or serve. Lounge cars are ornamented with scale models, speedometers, and allegorical panels depicting the histories of the railroads themselves and their pioneer achievements. Broad windows seek to give a maximum possible view of the passing landscape, the more immediate aspects of which are, inevitably, of a railroad significance. Time-tables are illustrated with

UP FROM THE OZARKS

The St. Louis, San Francisco Railway's No. 2, the Texas Special, with sixteen cars from San Antonio, Brownsville, Waco, Dallas, and Fort Worth, with de luxe chair-cars, standard Pullmans, valet, lounges, and diners, rolls up the Ozark miles to meet the sunrise sweeping across the Missouri meadows twenty-odd miles southwest of St. Louis. The Frisco is famous for the beauty and maintenance of its power, and this Mountain type No. 1504 is no exception with its red-painted bell mouth and number plate, trim valve gear, and silvered cylinder heads.

Lucius Beebe photograph

THESE MADE RAILROAD HISTORY

The first modern streamlined locomotive of conventional steam design in its essential internal economy was that which powered the Chicago, Milwaukee, St. Paul and Pacific's crack Hiawatha on the Chicago–Twin Cities run. It was a classic Atlantic type (4-4-2) fitted with a cowl of silver, black, and orange trim and was followed on the same run by heavier passenger power (4-6-4). The Hiawatha makes the 57.6 miles between Tower A-20 and Lake Forest in 38 minutes, or at a carded average of ninety miles an hour including the celebrated curve at Deerfield marked on the driver's instructions: "Reduce to 90." This is part of

Lucius Beebe photograph

the 75-minute, 85-mile run on which these steam-powered streamliners often hit over 100. Passenger service between Chicago and Milwaukee is among the fastest in the country, although up to January 2, 1935, competing roads, by the terms of a "gentleman's agreement" restricted speeds to 105 minutes over-all time. On the date the Chicago and North Western jumped the gun with its Twin Cities 400 with 75 minutes running time, the Milwaukee was forced to counter with no fewer than four expresses meeting the time cards of their rival. The Milwaukee, in 1941, had twenty-five expresses on this haul, the North Western, twenty-one, and the North Shore, thirty-six. The two Hiawathas were photographed by the author within a few miles of Lake Forest, Illinois.

DOLL HOUSE TRAIN

The Denver and Rio Grande Western's Prospector is probably the world's smallest standard-gage luxury train. In service overnight between Denver and Salt Lake by way of the fabled Moffat Route across the Continental Divide, this two-car unit provides in miniature most of the facilities found in seventeen-car varnish hauls such as the Century and the Chief. The units are Budd built and powered with horizontal Diesel engines slung beneath the cars. Because of the more than two per cent grades encountered in the Colorado Rockies, power rather than speed was the aim of its designers, although on its test run over the Reading in New Jersey it developed eighty-five miles an hour. There is room for more than 2000 pounds of headend revenue cargo, coach accommodations for forty-four passengers and sleeping space, in open berths and two drawing rooms, for eighteen. A tiny dinette seats eight and a minuscule observation lounge and solarium has space for four. Kitchen, offices, retiring rooms, and luggage lockers are included in its economy, and equalizers assure constant horsepower, light, and heat at all altitudes.

THE SUPER CHIEF

THE PANAMA LIMITED

All-Pullman, extra-fare, de luxe pride of the Illinois Central passenger fleet is the Panama Limited which leaves Chicago at one in the afternoon and pulls into New Orleans, 921 miles away, at nine the next morning. Its consist is pleasantly old fashioned with standard-weight Pullmans and non-revenue cars and its food is celebrated for its authentic Creole overtones, its generosity and expert service. Here the Panama Limited, powered by a Mountain locomotive, No. 2408, is southbound near Centralia, Illinois, at approximately fifty miles an hour.

SPEED FOR THE BANKERS AND BROKERS

The mainline of the Reading–Central of New Jersey–Baltimore and Ohio at Roselle, New Jersey, is six tracks deep, and over the fast iron the Reading's Seven O'Klocker, freighted with business men from Philadelphia, Trenton, and the Jersey countryside, thunders toward the Jersey City terminal at seventy-five miles an hour. This early morning flyer, running with no head-end traffic, carries coaches, a diner, and a club car and is powered by a well-shopped Pacific, No. 179, a locomotive similar to that which—redesigned with a stainless steel sheathing— hauls the streamliner, Crusader, over the same run twice a day each way.

Upper right: Lucius Beebe photograph

IN THE VALE OF BETHEL

The Central Vermont's Ambassador powered by a rebuilt super 4-8-2, No. 601, on the Montreal-Boston run, makes up time on the downgrade in the Vale of Bethel, Vermont.

Lower right: Railroad Photogra

ON THE BANKS OF THE OHIO

Primarily and highly profitably a coal haul road whose revenues largely derive from the mine regions of West Virginia, the Chesapeake and Ohio still runs three crack strings of varnish on the Washington–St. Louis haul with Pennsylvania connections for New York. The line is proud to refer to itself as "George Washington's Railroad," is justifiably fond of touting the food on its diners; is celebrated for its promotional cat Chessie, who sleeps like a kitten in thousands of yearly advertisements. This is the C. & O.'s Fast Flying Virginian, familiarly the F. F. V., tooling along near the Ohio River a few miles west of Huntington, West Virginia. Residents along the line are accustomed to set their watches by the daily passage of the F. F. V., the Sportsman, and the flagship of the fleet, the George Washington.

THE CENTRAL'S SOUTHWESTERN

With a white feather of steam at its stack and a pillar of soft coal smoke to mark its passing, the New York Central's Southwestern Limited on the New York–St. Louis run hits seventy on the speedway leading down to Granite City in southern Illinois. The power is a conventional Central Hudson, No. 5336.

Lucius Beebe photograph

IN THE LEGENDARY SIERRAS

Near Truckee, California, thirty-odd miles west of Reno, the Southern Pacific's cab-first, Baldwin-built articulated 4-8-8-2, No. 4181, thunders into the High Sierras with the Pacific Limited on the Chicago–San Francisco run by way of the Chicago and North Western, Union Pacific and Espee. The locomotive is of the Class AC-8, has 63½-inch drivers, a boiler pressure of 250 pounds and a tractive force of 124,300 pounds. Cab-first locomotives are indigenous to the Southern Pacific which originally designed them for operation exclusively between Roseville and Sparks, where snow sheds make visibility difficult and tunnels caused hardship and inconvenience from smoke exhaust and fumes to the crews of conventional engines. Now, however, the road uses them over many divisions, notably the San Joaquin and over the Siskiyou and Cascade ranges in northern California.

COVERS THE OLD WILD WEST

Three times a week during the summer months the Colorado and Southern runs No. 26, the Buffalo Bill, between Cody, Wyoming, and Denver by way of Thermopolis, Cheyenne, Fort Collins, and Boulder, names perfumed with the legends of the old frontier. Here is the Buffalo Bill behind a C. & S. light Pacific streaking into Denver on the advertised of a hot July noon.

Lucius Beebe photograph

RIO GRANDE LOCAL

Traveling across the Colorado meadows like the proverbial bat out of hell is this little local between Colorado Springs and Denver with a mail-storage car, two coaches, and a Pullman lounge. The engine, a light Pacific, No. 802, with more than the usual quota of sand domes, was doing an easy seventy when the picture was taken near Larkspur. The train is Rio Grande No. 10.

THE ROBERT E. LEE

Train No. 5 on the Seaboard Railway is the Robert E. Lee on the Washington-Birmingham run. Behind locomotives 208 and 213, both Mountain-type hogs, it is here rolling southward with green flags on either side of the engine stacks near Atlanta, Georgia, and with fourteen cars as the consist of its first section.

Upper right: Richard E. Prin photograph

CRACK TEXAN FLYER

is the Texas and Pacific's Sunshine Special which runs from St. Louis over the Missouri Pacific as far as Texarkana where its consist is taken over by the T. & P. for the run south. Its various sections serve Fort Worth and Dallas while through cars continue over the iron of the Southern Pacific from El Paso to Los Angeles and San Francisco. Specially designated locomotives serve this de luxe train on all divisions, and its make-up includes luxury cars of all classes, valets, shower baths, radios, soda fountains, and other amenities of comfort. The North Texas section, shown here, is pulling out for Dallas from the Fort Worth Yards behind Mountain type locomotive No. 902.

Lower right: Lucius Beebe photograph

THE GOLDEN STATE LIMITED

Behind one of the Rock Island Lines' Class M-50 Mountain-type locomotives, No. 4060, rolls the Golden State Limited with ten cars near Bureau Junction, Illinois, on its westward run. The Golden State runs daily between Chicago and Los Angeles over the Rock Island's iron to Tucumcari, New Mexico, where it joins the Southern Pacific. Complete with barber, showers, maid and valet service, radio, and ladies' lounge, it is a luxury train of note and specially favored by travelers who prefer a leisurely transcontinental trip by way of the southern route.

CARRYING WHITE ON THE M. & ST. L.

This heavy-duty Minneapolis and St. Louis 4-6-0, specially spruced up for the occasion and carrying the white flags of a special above its smokebox is on the head of an American Legion train rolling through the city center of Peoria, Illinois. The M. & St. L. is primarily a freight road but it has unearthed some old-time wooden coaches for the occasion which probably pleased the boys, off on a convention junket, just as much as modern streamlined equipment would have.

"SHE WAS WORKING STEAM WITH HER BRAKE SHOES SLACK"

With the Hudson Highlands and a bay of the Hudson River for a background, the Twentieth Century Limited is thundering down the dawn at Garrison, New York, before the era of the streamlined units which now comprise the most famous train in the world. The Hudson locomotive No. 5412 was then, as it still is, the archetypal passenger power on the New York Central's main line between Harmon, New York, and Chicago. Modifications in its essential economy, even in the latest streamlined models have been of minor consequence. The classification of this engine on the Central's power roster is J-3a.

HOW TIMES DO CHANGE!

The location of this early action shot and the name of the photographer are lost in obscurity, but the date is 1911 and the engine is a Canadian Pacific 4-6-0 with a consist of two mail and express cars, and three wooden coaches. This type of power hauled C. P. passenger trains across the continent in five or six days at that time and were considered the last word in design, efficiency, and speed.

Upper right:
William Barhar
Collection

MONSTER OF THE COAL PITS

The Pennsylvania is not often thought of by railroaders as a road favoring articulated locomotives, although a number of eastern companies which handle large tonnages of coal, notably the Western Maryland, Chesapeake and Ohio, Virginian, and Delaware and Hudson, have numbers of them in their roundhouses. The Pennsy, however, has a few listed on its power roster in varying wheel arrangements: 2-8-8-0 and 0-8-8-0, an example of the latter of which, Class CC-2-s is shown in action on a 4000-ton coal train out of Columbus, Ohio. All the road's articulated steam power operates in this neighborhood.

Lower right:
Railroad
Photographs

MODIFICATION ON THE UNION PACIFIC

North of Sand Creek, Colorado, the U. P.'s National Parks Special with Pacific No. 2906 on the head end, hits a mile a minute. This type of traditional locomotive with a "modernized" shroud built over it was first used by the U. P. on the streamlined, de luxe Chicago–San Francisco flyer, the Forty-Niner. No great shakes esthetically in the light of later design, it was one of the first reconditioned steam locomotives aimed at capturing the popular imagination.

maps and altitude charts and brochures emphasizing the advantages and pleasures of rail travel. Rapid successions of regional dishes on the menu (a traveler may start across the continent with Philadelphia scrapple and in rapid sequence encounter New York State cheese, Lake Superior white fish, fresh Iowa corn, Rocky Mountain trout, and the fresh figs and giant cracked crab of the Pacific Coast) serve to dramatize the speed of his going. Whether he be dining, drinking, sleeping, working, or simply loafing in a club car, no attempt is made to conceal from the passenger that he is on a train.

There are, also, happily a few exceptions to the general trend toward what is widely known as "modernism" in train decoration still discernible amidst a widespread urgency of chromium finish, straight lines, pastel colors, photomurals, and fluorescent lighting. All these devices recommend themselves without exception to railroad interiors, and their integrated ingenuity, utility, and harmonious esthetic effects are as flattering to the public taste as they are to the talents of the designers and construction engineers who have brought them into being. But the standard Pullman sleeping-car of thirty years ago with its green-curtained aisles, the vague and mysterious jungle life of its midnight corridors, its spacious drawing-rooms and general atmosphere of substantially upholstered luxury is too much of an American institution to be allowed altogether to vanish from the transportation scene in favor of all-room trains, roomettes, duplexes, and the super de luxe beauty of master suites such as those aboard the Century and Broadway. The up-to-the-minute single bedroom, most in demand of all Pullman sleeping arrangements, is unquestionably a vast improvement over the green carpeted ladder, the contortionist poses for trouser removal, and hopeless feeling of irrevocable isolation characteristic of the upper berth of tradition. But the traveler who has not groped blindly for his morning boots, has not encountered the curiosa of masculine undergarments on view in the matutinal men's wash room and finally emerged into the breakfast car, scarred with razor nicks stanched with fragments of toilet paper, but unquestionably victorious over a number of the major problems of civilization, has not seen life.

There are a variety of overland approaches to the Creole plaisances of

New Orleans ranging from the streamlined magnificence of the Southern Belles out of Kansas City on the Kansas City Southern–Louisiana and Arkansas, to the Louisiana Limited of the Texas and Pacific from the cities of East Texas, but if one is approaching the city of Antoine's and the Absinthe House from Chicago and the north, the Illinois Central's Panama Limited should be his choice. The Panama Limited is a noble train in the old manner, a luxurious, extra-fare, overnight flyer with equipment dating from somewhere along the time of the first World War and service that isn't surpassed on any silver and lacquered transcontinental thunderbolt of the immediate to-day. Its cars are standard Pullman sleepers, bedroom and stateroom accommodations, its brass railed observation lounge a miracle of fumed oak and Turkey carpets, and its diner a sort of mobile synthesis of Harvey's in Washington, Locke-Ober's in Boston, the aforementioned Antoine's, and all the good, old fashioned substantial restaurants of the countryside.

The Panama Limited holds no truck with thirty-cent breakfasts and sixty-cent dinners. Rather it runs to menus printed on gold finished stock, a profusion of costly cut flowers, specially designed English silver and Czecho-Slovakian service, and a cuisine which entirely complements the other excellences of its appointments. The Panama Limited is the very archetype of luxury railroading before shotwelding and articulated cars were dreamed of and deserves to be preserved in service as an eloquent souvenir of heartier times and more spacious tastes in comfort.

In the transition stage between the standard-weight Pullman smart train of yesterday and the most modern imaginable examples of Pullman and luxury coach varnish hauls such as the Southern Railway's Southerner and Tennessean, the El Capitans on the Sante Fe and the latest additions to the Rock Island's spectacular fleet of Rockets, is one of the earliest of long run Diesel-electric speedsters, still considered by many among the most beautiful of all streamliners—the Burlington's Denver Zephyr. The Denver Zephyr was placed in revenue service in 1936 with a daily run between Chicago and Denver of 1036 miles and has an on-time percentage on this third-of-a-continent run at an average of sixty-five miles an hour of 91 per cent. A highly individualistic streak of silver racing across the Colorado uplands, the Zephyr's apartments are slightly smaller than those on light-weight trains of later design, but it is easily one of the most handsomely appointed in the land. Its drawing-rooms and compartments in addition to complete thermal control, boast individual electric clocks exactly synchronized, radio sets, and a harmony of decorative schemes and fabric materials of great variety.

In the far West the ultimate in upholstered daylight runs is supplied by the Southern Pacific's new Daylight equipment, designed to make the Los Angeles–San Francisco trip over the Coast Route even more luxurious for the most fastidious passenger, while on the night run over the same iron there are the new streamlined Larks built by Southern Pacific and the Pullman Company at a cost in excess of $2,600,000.

Each train has seventeen cars, including twelve sleepers, a combination sleeper-café-lounge car, diner, lounge, and two baggage cars. Still under construction are the two "triplex units" consisting of a lounge car, diner, and kitchen car, which will replace the present improved diners and lounges, increasing to eighteen the number of cars to a single train.

Featuring room accommodations exclusively, each train has seven drawing-rooms, thirteen compartments, ninety-one double bedrooms and fifty roomettes, with capacity for a maximum of 270 persons. Exterior color of the trains is two-tone gray with aluminum striping. Soft shades of brown and blue predominate in the interior color scheme, with furnishings to match.

Out of the Company's shops at Sacramento came four of the headend postal and baggage cars, completely redesigned, streamlined, and painted for exclusive use on these new trains.

The Larks are the senior trains on the coast run between San Francisco and Los Angeles, the original trains of that name having gone into service May 8, 1910. In the succeeding years they gained a reputation as one of the outstanding de luxe trains in the United States, a distinction they share to-day with the Daylights on the daytime run.

Worthy of notice as a most significant development in high-grade accommodations for railroad passenger travel has been the emergence during the past several years of a number of de luxe all-coach trains on long distance and transcontinental runs. Time was when coach traffic wasn't accorded much attention by railway managements and when it was felt that the ever diminishing returns from this particular source of revenue might eventually, save in the case of commuter traffic, warrant its suspension entirely. But the discovery by a few pioneering traffic managers that, with an improvement of service, accommodations, and schedules and the creation of new forms of promotion and passenger appeal, the swiftly vanishing coach traffic could be turned into an amazingly profitable source of revenue.

For the pleasure and satisfaction of long-haul coach passengers, most of them riding at reduced fares, there was suddenly recruited a corps of car designers, decorative experts, dieticians, hostesses, and other experts and functionaries whose energies were solely concerned for the recapture of this type of passenger as a patron of the railroads. And there came into being a fleet of long-distance flyers whose only accommodations were luxury coaches and the accustomed non-revenue cars. Notable among them were the Santa Fe's El Capitans on the Chicago–California run, the first coach trains in history to charge an actual extra fare, the Pennsylvania's Trail Blazer, and the Central's Pathfinder, each in the New York–Chicago service, the Pennsylvania's Jeffersonian on the New York–St. Louis run, the Atlantic Coast Line's Vacationer, the Seaboard's Silver Meteors, the Florida and East Coast's Champions in the New York–Florida service, the Southern's Tennessean and Southerner in service between Washington and the deep South, and the Chicago and Eastern Illinois' Henry M. Flagler, the Illinois Central's City of Miami and the Pennsylvania's South Wind between Chicago and Florida during the winter season, and the Pennsylvania's East Wind on schedule between Washington and Portland, Maine, during the summer season.

Characteristic of most of these trains, especially those on the Florida runs, has been Diesel-electric motive-power. The Jeffersonian, Pathfinder, Trail Blazer, the East Wind and South Wind and the Chicago and Eastern Illinois Florida streamliner are steam powered over the greater part of their runs. All have embodied undreamed-of conveniences in coach travel: reclining chair seats, individual reading lights and universal fluorescent illumination, elaborate photomurals and photomontage arranged by distinguished decorators, special cars for women

"IN THAT NEW WORLD WHICH IS THE OLD
AND O'ER THE HILLS AND FAR AWAY!"

Behind a thundering road engine and a helper, a 4-8-2 and 4-8-4 respectively, the Southern Pacific No. 1, the Sunset Limited Westbound, heads into the last lap of the transcontinental haul from New Orleans to Los Angeles with seventeen cars of mail, coaches, and Pullmans. The helper was picked up at Indio, California, an Espee division point, and both hoggers will be working steam until they reach Palm Springs where the grade is downward to Banning and Redlands.

BELLE OF THE SOUTH

Posing for its picture is the Kansas City Southern–Louisiana and Arkansas Southern Belle, Diesel-electric four-car pacemaker on the run between Kansas City and New Orleans. The single-unit 2000-horsepower locomotive was built by Electro-Motive, the cars were designed and built by the Pullman-Standard Car Manufacturing Company. Notable for the harmony of its decorative scheme the Southern Belle emphasizes the railroad industry in the murals of its observation lounge cars, the subject in one of its units, shown opposite, being the Kansas City terminal depot and in the other a pair of giant K. C. S.–L. & A. Northern locomotives leaving a roundhouse.

Pullman photograph

IN THE MODERN MANNER

The Pullman-Standard Car Manufacturing Company designed and built this observation lounge for the Kansas City Southern–Louisiana and Arkansas Railway Companies' Southern Belle and included in its economy every known refinement of decoration and comfort. The photomural shows the railroad terminal at Kansas City, famed for its Harvey Restaurant, its populous bar, and its elaborate bookshop. Like St. Louis and Chicago, Kansas City is very railroad conscious, and no small amount of its business and social life revolves around the depot.

Lucius Beebe photograph

HEADED FOR FAR HORIZONS

The West Texas Section of the Texas and Pacific's Sunshine Limited pulls out of Fort Worth on the El Paso run in a cloud of steam exhaust as the hogger notches back his throttle and adjusts his Johnson bar for the first leg of the long pull across the desert wastes of the Lone Star State.

THE BROADWAY COMES HOME

Over the four tracks of the Pennsylvania's mainline between New York and Philadelphia rolls unceasingly, day and night, year in and year out, the heaviest freight and passenger traffic in the world. Popular legend has it that at Monmouth Junction, New Jersey, there is a train passing every four and a half minutes, although verification of such a belief without actual timing over an extended period would be difficult in the light of the scores of daily extras scheduled over this division. Shown here is the Broadway Limited, crack, extra-fare Pennsy lace curtains between Chicago and New York, coming down the home stretch near Rahway, New Jersey. On the head end is Westinghouse Electric engine No. 4999, Class R-1, an experimental locomotive with a 4-8-4 wheel arrangement, 18,750 pounds' tractive effort at 90 miles an hour, and solid trucks instead of the more customary articulated type. Specially maintained and painted for service on the Broadway between Harrisburg and Manhattan, it is the only engine of its class in service on the system.

Lucius Beebe photograph

DRIFTING INTO PALM SPRINGS

Against a grim background of California mountains and ahead of a heavy consist of Christmas mail and express in addition to the regular passenger accommodations, the Southern Pacific's Sunset Limited, eastbound, is double heading up the stiff grade between Banning and Palm Springs. A moment before both of these typical Espee Mountain type locomotives had been working steam with their Johnson bars in the corner, but the momentum of eighteen standard weight steel cars is sufficient to allow their hoggers to drift the last half mile into the well-designed Mission style station at the famed desert resort.

RACING FOR CHICAGO

Running southward toward Chicago on the iron of the Chicago and North Western is the Soo Dominion Line's Mountaineer powered by a North Western 4-6-2 as it tops seventy through Lake Forest, Illinois. The Mountaineer is the Soo Line's daily varnish between Chicago and the North Pacific Coast, running part of the way over the rails of the North Western, over the Soo's own right-of-way to Portal and via Canadian Pacific to Vancouver. Its consist includes solarium lounge cars, diners, bedroom sleepers, tourist sleepers, and coaches.

Upper right:
Lucius Beebe
photograph

MOPAC SUPERPOWER

Company built, this extraordinarily handsome Mountain type Missouri Pacific engine No. 5321 is highballing with No. 12, the Scenic Limited at fifty miles an hour, eastbound at Kirkwood, Missouri. The Scenic is heading in from Kansas City with cars from Salt Lake, Pueblo, and Denver.

Lower right:
William Barham
—Ivan Oaks
photograph

FULL OF YEARS AND HONORS

The Lehigh Valley has recently modernized three of its most notable passenger trains, the Asa Packer, the John Wilkes and the long famous Black Diamond which runs daily both ways between New York and Buffalo. The Black Diamond was placed in service in May, 1896, and so is the senior of the Broadway and the Century and most of the other distinguished cross-continent streaks of varnish. Among the trains which have been in service continually for a greater length of time than the Black Diamond are the Pennsylvania's Congressional Limited on the Washington–New York run, and the Florida Special in service between New York and Miami on the timetables of the Atlantic Coast Line. The Florida Special was placed in operation in 1886. In 1940 the Black Diamond was streamlined but the action photograph here shows it with standard equipment wheeling through Bound Brook, New Jersey, behind a massive Northern type engine on the morning run westward.

Lucius Beebe photograph

ALONG THE ALTON

The Alton Limited on the Chicago–St. Louis run, shown here behind Pacific No. 5296 near Springfield, Illinois, usually runs with a slightly larger consist than the rival Wabash Banner Blue or C. & E. I. Zipper, as it carries a through sleeper bound for Oklahoma City on the Frisco's No. 9. Here its consist includes five revenue cars, a lounge, diner, and head-end revenue mail-storage car.

Lucius Beebe photograph

K4S IN MODERN DRESS

Close on the westering markers of the all-Pullman Spirit of St. Louis, the Pennsylvania's de luxe flyer on the New York–St. Louis run, follows the almost equally luxurious all-coach, streamlined, up-to-the-minute Jeffersonian. The power is one of the Pennsy's GG 1 electrics from New York to Harrisburg, a classic K4s of familiar design from Harrisburg to Pittsburgh, and from there to St. Louis the train is hauled by such handsomely refurbished K4s models as this, completely modernized with nickel-steel cylinder heads, silver-trimmed headlamp and handrails, solid steel pilot with retractable coupling, airflow boiler lagging, and generous trim of brilliant crimson on keystone, nameplate, and tender. The engines represent the most radical departure from accepted Pennsylvania design in years and have attracted widespread enthusiasm from trainmen, amateurs, and passengers. Here is the Jeffersonian hitting close to eighty approximately fifteen miles out of East St. Louis on the westbound run.

R. H. Kindig photograph

AMONG THE LATTER-DAY SAINTS

The Chicago and North Western–Union Pacific–Southern Pacific's most exquisitely appointed transcontinental streamliner, the City of San Francisco, on the Chicago–San Francisco run, drifts down Echo Canyon, Utah, behind Diesel-electric units SF 1, 2, 3 with their potential total of 5400 horsepower.

MAIN LINE WEST

About 1905, when this photograph was taken, the Twentieth Century Limited was the last word in overland travel but its regular consist of five cars would look small compared to the Century's string of fifteen or sixteen cars to-day. The photograph, strangely enough showing left-hand operation, was taken on the mainline of the Lake Shore and Michigan Southern (New York Central System) somewhere between Cleveland and Chicago with a high-wheeled and speedy 4-6-0 on the headend.

New York Central photograph

Lucius Beebe photograph

SERVICE FOR THE CHIEF

At Las Vegas, New Mexico, the Atchison, Topeka and Santa Fe's crack, extra-fare limited on the Chicago–Los Angeles run, pauses briefly for fuel and servicing. Here a yard worker is lubricating the main pin of the Chief's mighty Northern type locomotive which powers the train on the entire run from La Junta, Colorado, to the Pacific Coast. The grease gun he holds is actuated by air pressure piped from the cock on the tank overhead, and his supply of grease cartridges is slung over his shoulder much as ammunition is carried for an automatic rifle.

BIG POWER FOR THE BIG FOUR

The New York Central System's (Big Four Route) Missourian on the Cleveland–St. Louis run is eating up the miles in southern Illinois behind a Hudson, the equipment of which includes a large feed water heater hung forward of its smokebox. The road's crack train on this run is the Southwestern Limited although the most direct route is that of the Pennsylvania which has also the advantage of modern streamlined equipment on both its Spirit of St. Louis and all-coach luxury train, the Jeffersonian.

Paul H. Stringham photograph

THE VANISHING TEN-WHEELER

as exemplified by the Nickel Plate Road's No. 156 hauling the Peoria to Frankfort, Illinois, local passenger train across Farm Creek Bridge, just east of Peoria at sixty miles an hour.

NEARING ITS TERMINAL

On the four-track mainline of the Boston and Albany near Faneuil station, Massachusetts, the New York Central's Boston–Chicago flyer, the New England States, is within a few miles of its eastern terminal. From Albany to Boston it is powered by a B. & A. Hudson, reminiscent in almost every detail of design except its square sand dome, of the Hudsons of the parent road, the Central. The New England States is an all-Pullman de luxe train taking the place of the old Boston section of the Twentieth Century Limited which, with its extra fare, was never a great favorite with thrifty Yankee passengers. The substitute New England States, however, runs daily in heavy sections of sixteen and seventeen cars and is one of the B. & A.'s and Central's profitable passenger hauls.

Upper right:
Lucius Beebe
photograph

LOUISVILLE AND NASHVILLE MIKE

Probably the Mikado is still the most widely listed freight locomotive on the power rosters of the nation's railroads. From one seacoast to the other and from Canada to the Rio Grande it is the commonplace of daily despatching, the engine of all work. This Louisville and Nashville 2-8-2 is running ahead of Train 85, the Bullet, eastbound through the Illinois countryside near Belleville at forty miles an hour. Note the engine numbers on the headlight glass for night identification, an L. & N. characteristic and identifying mark.

Lower right:
William Barham
—Ivan Oaks
photograph

TYPICAL OF CANADIAN RAILROADING

is this striking shot of the Canadian Pacific's Dominion, breasting the grade at Dead Man's Curve, Yoho, British Columbia. The closed-in cabs on the engines are necessary in a country where below-zero temperatures and severe blizzards characterize winter runs on every division of the system.

HEADED SOUTH RAPIDLY

is the Fort Worth and Denver (Burlington) Texas Zephyr at Castle Rock, Colorado. Behind a gleaming double Diesel-electric unit are coaches, Pullmans, and non-revenue cars for Oklahoma and the deep southwest as far as Houston, San Antonio, and New Orleans. What once was the Fort Worth and Denver is operated by Colorado and Southern for the "Q," and the Zephyr is the crack varnish on the daily run in each direction.

and children alone, registered nurse and hostess service, washrooms of standard Pullman dimensions, lounge cars of luxurious appointments with radios and other amusement facilities, and restaurant cars with comprehensive menus with moderate-priced combination meals.

There remains for brief consideration the group of super de luxe, extra fare, transcontinental glamour trains which, although their clientèle is necessarily limited, have laid such a hold upon the public imagination and which by reason of their surcharges, capacity bookings during seasonal periods, and extensive headend revenue, are extremely profitable items in the catalogue of railroad properties. They include the Twentieth Century Limited and Broadway Limited, top notch, rights-over-all varnish thunderbolts of the Central and Pennsylvania between New York and Chicago, the Chicago and North Western–Union Pacific's City of Los Angeles, the Chicago and North Western–Union Pacific–Southern Pacific's City of San Francisco and Forty-Niner, and the Santa Fe's Chief and Super Chief. All of these are trains of light-weight, airflow construction, and, generally speaking, their motive-power is about equally divided between steam and Diesel-electric.

In the esteem of the author, the Broadway is the handsomest light-weight train on any run. Pullman built, designed and decorated by Raymond Loewy, its murals and decorative motifs, its characteristic Pennsylvania Tuscan red exteriors, historical panels, walls of rare inlaid woods and handsome fabrics would seem to constitute the ultimate in flagship luxury.

Scarcely less eye-filling, the Century has for forty years been celebrated in song and story, fiction, film, stage drama, verse, legend, and even music as the most famous train on earth. Notable among world travelers and amateurs of fine living are its twin dining-cars, complete as any metropolitan restaurant with private apartments, three distinctive changes of table linen for each run, fluorescent lighting, dinner-jacketed maîtres d'hôtel, subdued string music, and comprehensive menus. There is probably more champagne drunk on the Century than on any train in America and, late in the evening, after the service of dinner, the restaurant cars are translated into night clubs through the medium of an entire change of service, menu, lighting effects, and music.

The City of Los Angeles is notable principally for its seventeen-car consist, the largest of any train of its type, its sailing list of stage and film celebrities and its Little Nugget Bar, a gilt and ormolu replica of an opulent California tavern during gold rush days and complete with canaries in gilded cages, red plush, fringed and looped portieres, floriated electroliers, and marquetry tables. The new City of San Francisco is of much the same design, lacking only the florid touch of the Little Nugget with its romantic and bonanza overtones.

The Chief and Super Chief, flashing between Chicago and Los Angeles over the legendary Santa Fe Trail, across the mountains of Colorado and New Mexico and the deserts of Arizona and California, probably play as prominent a part in the film saga of Hollywood as the names of Pickford, Paramount, or De Mille. Both trains, the Chief daily, the Super Chief twice a week, are freighted with the glamorous and exploited of the celluloid world and their attendant literary and financial luminaries. The Harvey dining-car service of the Santa Fe is an American institution, and the menu of the Super Chief is a sort of synthesis of those of New York's Colony, Chicago's Pump Room and the much touted steak houses of Kansas City.

The cars of the Super Chief are of standard construction, tailored by the Edward G. Budd Manufacturing Company, Philadelphia.

The decorative motif is in a sense a memorial to some of the original inhabitants of the lands which were granted to the railroad in the middle of the last century—to the Navajos. Color schemes, designs, and aspects of their art are used and developed in a beautiful and restrained fashion in portions of the train. In the place of the traditional green upholstery and red paint surfaces, there is in the Super Chief rare and lovely wood paneling and a wide variety of upholstering such as one would wish to have in one's home. The woods used came from the four corners of the earth—teak from Burma and burl heart of the California redwood, zebra wood from Africa, and a score of other kinds. Wherever one's glance falls, from beginning to end of the train, there is something lovely and something interesting to look at and to enjoy. In the upholstery there are rich and soft colors, such as desert gold, ash rose, or cerulean blue. Painted surfaces and metal trimmings highlight the effect of the fine woods and the rich fabrics. Deep piled carpets cover the train's entire floor. Lighting is indirect and fixtures are of restrained modern design.

It would be possible to continue almost indefinitely with a catalogue of the features of the daily and overnight luxury trains which annually roll up millions of passenger miles between the Atlantic and the Pacific: the restaurant car of the Forty-Niner which was once the private saloon car of a Mexican president, the streamlined magnificence of the new Empire State Express, a far cry from its wooden coaches of the record year of 1893, the wine card of the Merchants Limited and Yankee Clipper of the New Haven, the most extensive known, the nickel steel and red trim glory of the converted K-4s Pacifics which power the Jeffersonian, the operations schedule which makes possible the record speed of the Congressional Limited between Washington and New York, the inordinately handsome red and silver coaches of the James Whitcomb Riley, the multitudinous bars, lounges, counter lunches and formal diners of the Daylight.

But space is urgent and brevity is of the essence. As with Sir Christopher Wren's inscription in St. Paul's—*Si Monumentum Requiris, Circumspice*—so if one requires a monument to the genius of American railroading, let him travel by railroad.

Lucius Beebe photograph

(1)